FOR STARTERS

An introduction to Christianity to help those who are seriously interested - for use at a personal, one-to-one, or group level.

23 STUDIES

With questions answered,
challenges to think about
and suggested Bible readings.

IMPORTANT NOTE

These pages are bound and punched in such a way that individual Study, Question and Challenge pages can be removed and kept in an A4 Ring file, if so desired, allowing flexibility of use.

GRACE PUBLICATIONS TRUST
139 Grosvenor Avenue
London, N5 2NH
England

Managing Editors
J. P. Arthur M.A.
H. J. Appleby

ISBN 0 946462 44 5
© Clifford Pond 1997

Distributed by
EVANGELICAL PRESS
12 Wooler Street
Darlington
Co. Durham DL1 1RQ
England

Scripture quotations, unless otherwise indicated, are taken from the Holy
Bible, New International Version, Copyright © 1973, 1978, 1984 by International Bible Society. Used by permission of Hodder and Stoughton, a
member of the Hodder Headline Group.

Cover design by L.L. Evans
Layout and typesetting by Jonathan Smith, Potton, Beds.
Printed in Great Britain

CONTENTS

INTRODUCTION

Let's Go !   You are seriously interested in Christianity but you have got stuck in a jam somewhere along the road. Here is something to get you moving

Where to ?   A discovery   —   of what Christianity is
                                  —   of how to become a Christian
                                  —   of the Christian life

How ?   By using the Bible. You can only know what Christianity is from the Bible, so do not get side-tracked with guesses no matter how fascinating

What route ?   By way of twenty three studies each of which is divided into 3 sections

The study itself   what the Bible says is the most important thing, so read the references carefully

Note: If you are not used to the Bible

— you will find the key to book name abbreviations in the appendices

— you will soon find your way around as you search for the texts in each study

Questions	–	Clues to answers to questions often asked; most of the questions need more complete answers but these clues will point you in the right direction
		it is right to ask questions, but be willing to accept what the Bible says – don't probe into questions the Bible does not answer
Challenges	–	these will help you apply the study to yourself; be sure to give honest answers why not write them down in your own notebook? – tackle as many as your time will allow

NOW GET GOING!

STUDY I
HOW TO READ THE BIBLE

Reading: *Psalm 119: 97-104*

(**Note:** law, commands, statutes etc describe different aspects of the Bible)

v 97   Our progress in understanding the Bible depends on how much we
                love the truth and how much time we give to thinking about it.

vv 98-100   We need to beware of being proud about our knowledge of the
                Bible, and yet not to be over-awed by people who may try to force
                their views on us with their apparently superior knowledge.

vv 101-102   The true test of understanding is not in head knowledge but in
                obedience. Spiritual knowledge must result in holy living.

vv 103   If we really love God we will not read the Bible as a
                duty or habit, but as something that gives us great pleasure.

**Reading the Bible teaches us what God wants us to do and
gives us the desire to do it.**

" O God please teach me to read and understand the Bible and help
me do what it says."

**Everything that follows in this manual is based on the Bible –
Why?**

Because the Bible is not man's search for God but God's
truth given to us; it comes to us with his authority.   2 Peter 1:16-21

*"All Scripture is God-breathed and is useful for teaching,
rebuking, correcting and training in righteousness,
so that the man of God may be thoroughly equipped
for every good work." (2 Tim. 3:16-17)*

We read books in different ways – we read a book of poems in a different way from a telephone directory: or a novel from a DIY manual

 ## So how should we read the Bible?

- Read it **regularly** – this is spiritual food – neglect
  results in spiritual starvation

  Ps. 1:1-6
  Job 23:11-12
  1 Peter 2:1-3

- Read it **thoroughly** – the whole Bible is God's Word
  to us – so we need it all not just parts we like best – as
  with food for our bodies we need a balanced spiritual diet

  Josh. 1:7-9
  Ps. 119:9-11

- Read it **prayerfully** – before reading the Bible ask the
  Lord to show you the truth about himself, yourself, the
  world & especially what Jesus Christ has done, is doing
  and is going to do – pray that you will grow in
  knowledge and in love

  Ps. 119:18
  Luke 24:27
  Luke 24:44-47

- Read it **humbly** – because God is the author;
  remember to be patient; hold on to what you do
  understand and wait for further light on the difficult
  parts – remember to ask for help – that is why God
  gave us teachers – remember to be obedient –
  progress in the Christian life is as much dependant
  on obedience as it is on knowledge

  Isa. 66:1-2

  John 16:12-13
  Eph. 4:11-12
  Ps. 66:18
  John 7:17
  James 2:26

- Read it with **worship** – use the reading to stimulate your
  prayer & praise, thanksgiving, confession, love, faith & hope Col. 3:16-17

 " Dear God, thank you for the Bible; please speak to me through its teaching."

QUESTIONS ASKED ABOUT STUDY I

The Bible is a big book and parts of it are difficult to understand. Where do I begin?

Begin with the easier parts and gradually make inroads into the harder ones. There are some key passages that provide a kind of skeleton which will fill out as you go on. You will find a list of such passages in the **appendices** at the end of the manual; read through them at your own pace at least twice without explanatory notes, noticing the way the later passages build on the earlier ones. The idea is simply to become familiar with the contents, and then you could follow one of the Bible reading schemes with helpful comments. You will find a list of such schemes also in the **appendices.**

Why are there two parts to the Bible?

There is no direct answer to this question. We have to accept that this was God's way of making his truth known to us. The two Testaments do remind us that the Bible progresses from one stage to another like the growth of a child, or moving on from a blue print to the reality. Everything in the Old Testament points on to Jesus Christ. There we find prophets, priests and kings; these all foreshadow Jesus Christ who is the perfect prophet, priest and king. Also he fulfilled all the meaning of the sacrifices, offerings and feasts that were observed in Old Testament days (Luke 24:25-26; 44-47).

I find it difficult to concentrate on Bible reading and prayer. My mind wanders and I am easily distracted. How can I overcome this problem?

Are you using the best time and place? Change to a more suitable situation even if some much loved activity has to be put aside. Wandering thoughts can be captured by reading and praying aloud, or at least by silently 'mouthing' them. If you are afraid of forgetting something that has dropped into your mind, make a note of it and then get on with your devotions. If practical, it can help to read the Bible with a friend. Tell the Lord about your problem and tackle it with determination.

Which is the best version to use?

If you regularly attend a church, the version your church uses is probably the best for you. This will avoid confusion and give you continuity. The variations between the versions are not sufficient to affect any basic Christian teaching, so use the one you are most comfortable with.

QUESTIONS ASKED ABOUT STUDY 1

 I am so tired with the pressures of life, I go to sleep when I begin to read.

 Your spiritual life is so important you should ask yourself if you need to be so busy. Be willing to make a sacrifice for the sake of your spiritual growth. If your pressures are unavoidable, then follow the advice in the answer to question 3. Remember, your heavenly Father understands, so don't fret, but also remember if you are careless about this you will be the one who loses out.

 Why should I not just read the parts of the Bible I like and leave the rest?

 Because all the Bible is from God and all of it has important things to say to us about his truth and about the Christian life.

 Why should I bother with Bible reading notes? Surely I should rely on the Holy Spirit?

 We certainly need to ask the Holy Spirit to help our understanding, and reading notes should not distract us from the Bible itself. But most Christians find they are helped by a set scheme of daily readings and by notes written by respected Bible teachers. Why not adopt two methods? At one time of day read the Bible and meditate on it without notes, and at another time use one of the Bible reading schemes.

Note: We will discuss more questions about the Bible in **Study 5.**

CHALLENGES from STUDY 1

 What are the possible reasons why you will not read the Bible regularly?

 What is it about the Bible that appeals to you?

 What do you find most difficult about reading the Bible?

 Write down your plan for daily Bible reading — ask the Lord to help you to keep to it.

 Write down further questions on this subject you will ask your group leader or Christian friend.

ACTION

 Learn and/or write down 2 Timothy 3:16-17.
Learn the names and order of the books of the Bible.

STUDY 2
GOD BEGAN EVERYTHING

Reading: *Isaiah 40: 9-26*

v 9   God is very wonderful; we should not be ashamed of him, nor of telling others about him.

v 10-11   God is both mighty and merciful; it is important to give equal weight to both of these qualities. Because of his great strength he is able to be effective in his care for us, unlike idols that themselves have to be carried.

v 12-14   God is greater than his creation; he is not part of creation, but having made it he sustains and controls it.

v 15-17   God is greater than the nations; he cares for the nations but compared with him they are no greater than drops of water carelessly spilled from a bucket.

v 18-20   God cannot be compared with anything or anyone else. When we try to guess what God is like, we reach some very absurd conclusions.

v 21-26   Nothing exists that God has not made including every star and planet in space. Quite apart from what God tells us about himself in the Bible, a thoughtful consideration of the world we live in should convince us that God is very great.

> " O God, help me to understand how great you are."

Everything begins with God – creation, the human race, the Bible, the way we are put right with God.   Gen. 1:1

The best way to find answers to questions about the world and our lives, is always to put God first in our thinking

We can know about God, not by searching, but by receiving what he has told us about himself   Job 11:7-9

    in creation, *"The heavens declare the glory of God;*
        the skies proclaim the work of his hands." (Ps. 19:1)

        when we make things other people draw
        conclusions about us e.g. careless, clever,   Rom 1:18-20
        ignorant. In the same way we know some
        things about God from what he has made,
        e.g. his goodness, power, wisdom, love of beauty.

STUDY 2 Continued

in the Bible *"The LORD, the LORD, the compassionate and gracious God,*
slow to anger, abounding in love and faithfulness, maintaining
love to thousands, and forgiving wickedness, rebellion and sin.
Yet he does not leave the guilty unpunished;"(Exod. 34:6-7)

– creation by itself is not enough, the Bible tells us
more about what God is like – his sovereignty,
majesty, love, patience, hatred of evil, holiness.   1 John 4:7-10

in Jesus Christ   *"No-one has ever seen God, but God the only Son*
who is at the Father's side, has made him known." (John 1:18)

– he is the perfect and final revelation of God by his
life, teaching, miracles, death and resurrection.   John 17:1-6

What kind of being is God?

We know people in two ways – their appearance and their character.
We will consider God's character in **Study 3** – here are some things about
his 'appearance':

He is spirit – he does not have a physical body but he is not
a ghost, he is real   John 4:24

He is invisible – we cannot see him but he is seen by angelic
beings and Christians who have died   1 Tim. 1:17

He is a person – not merely a power, force or mind.   Ps. 115:1-8
He is able to love people, talk to them,   John 3:16
listen to them, reason with them   Isa. 1:18

He is distinct from what he made
– he is not 'Nature' - he is as separate from
creation and as superior to it as a woman is   Isa. 40:21-26
distinct from and superior to a dress she has made   Ps. 89:9-13

He is eternal – unlimited by time   Isa. 40:28

He can do anything – nothing is beyond his power   Luke 1:26-38;
Heb. 11:3

He knows everything – there is nothing, past, present or
future outside his knowledge   Ps. 139:1-16

He controls everything
– nothing happens by chance, he makes   Acts 17:24-25;
sure that everything occurs according   Rom. 11:33-36
to his plan and he keeps everything going

" Dear God, please show me how I can believe in you and trust you."

QUESTIONS ASKED ABOUT STUDY 2

Can you prove the existence of God?

The Bible does not set out to prove God's existence; it assumes this should be obvious. Christians sometimes point to the wonder, order and complexity of creation and the evidence of a designer as proof that God exists. This argument has limited value – it is better to begin with faith; when we do that everything else falls into place (Heb. 11:6).

Is evolution opposed to belief in God?

There is no contradiction between belief in God and the Bible, and proven facts about the world; evolution is by no means an established fact. Some Christians believe they can reconcile the teaching of Scripture with the theory of evolution.

However, the Bible seems clear that the world was made out of nothing (Ps. 33:6-9). Likewise the Bible teaches that the first man was made without any preliminary process. (Gen. 2:4-7; Heb. 11:3) If we begin with the eternal all-powerful God there is no difficulty in believing the Bible account of creation. Find a competent scientist who also accepts the Bible teaching – there are quite a lot of them around! Ask for advice about books by such people – there are plenty of those available too!

If the evidence for the existence of God is so clear, why do people generally reject it?

Because they 'suppress the truth' (Rom. 1:19-20) It is not because there is insufficient evidence, but men and women do not want to believe in God, so they suppress what they know instinctively is true. They know that belief in God will mean a change in their lives, and this they are unwilling to face. *" Once, in a very revealing admission, an Ivy League Physics Professor told me that his 'reason' for accepting a naturalistic perspective, was that 'it is ethically more comfortable to believe this way'. In fact, Julian Huxley admitted he received a great sense of relief in believing that God does not exist".* (Miracles & The Modern Mind, Norman L Geisler, Baker p41)

If God is in control of everything, is this the same as fate?

No. Because fate is an impersonal power but God rules the world with love and wisdom working to his own plan. Fate has no feeling – God has feelings of pain and pleasure about what he sees happening in the world (Isa. 63:7-9). If you are reluctant to accept the idea of God's control consider the alternatives. Would you prefer Satan to rule or man to rule? Is it more comforting to believe in chance where nothing is certain or in fate where everything is fixed no matter what we do? Or is it better to have a God who knows what he is doing and with whom we can talk?

QUESTIONS ASKED ABOUT STUDY 2

All religions believe in some kind of god. Are they not all basically the same?

Christianity stands on its own despite all the attempts to minimise the differences between the various religions.
The Christian God is unique – see **Study 4.**
The Christian way of peace is unique – see **Study 15.**

How can we believe in a God of love when the world is so full of cruelty and disasters?

The love of God still comes through clearly despite these things, which happen because of the entry of sin into the world– see **Study 7.**
God continues to provide for all the needs of mankind though many suffer because of man's greed and cruelty. God also provides the only real comfort for the victims of natural disasters either directly or through the compassion of others (Acts 11:27-30). Christians are distressed at the world's sufferings but their faith is not destroyed by them, because God has said they would happen (Matt. 24:6-7).

It is difficult to understand how God can be both a spirit and a person.

A person thinks, plans, loves, envies, hates, desires – we do all these things apart from our bodies. We are so used to our person being expressed through our bodies it is not easy to understand how a person can be expressed through a spirit being, especially when that being fills heaven and earth (Jer.23:24). If God were merely a physical body, he would be no greater than ourselves and if he were not a person, communication between him and us would be impossible. We accept both facts gratefully while acknowledging that it is a mystery beyond our understanding. We believe what he tells us about himself, and do not pry into things he has not told us. If we understood everything about God he would not be God.

QUESTIONS ASKED ABOUT STUDY 2

It is difficult to believe that one person could create the universe out of nothing.

It is not difficult to believe that the God of the Bible could do this. When we have an adequate view of God as all-powerful and all-wise, the Bible account of creation becomes credible. It is more reasonable to believe in a personal Creator than that the universe came into being by some chance happening. Make sure your God is not too small.

If God is in control of the world why has it become such a dangerous place with global warming and other causes for alarm?

Not all scientists share this alarm and we need to beware not to shape our thinking by human speculation. But there is no doubt that humans have abused the earth's resources driven by greed and lust for power resulting in an unfair distribution of God's good gifts. In the beginning man was told to "subdue" the earth (Gen. 1:26); this was not a licence to waste or hoard but to harness the resources for the good of all. If God were not in control there is no doubt mankind would have destroyed itself before now, but the end will not come until God's time – see **Studies 21-22**.

What makes Christianity different from other religions?

This is a good question because there is a widespread assumption that there are considerable similarities, but the differences are much greater. Here are some of them:

a)   Only Christianity has God who is both three and one – see **Study 4**

b)   Only Christianity depends on the continuing life and authority of its Founder and not only on teaching given in the past – see **Study 12**

c)   Only Christianity is rooted in historical events depending entirely on them (i.e: the life, death and resurrection of Jesus Christ – see **Studies 8-11**

d)   Only Christianity has God himself coming down to make himself known and to die for the benefit of his people.

e)   Only Christianity provides a cure for a guilty conscience. (Heb. 10:22)

f)   Only Christianity provides a way of salvation that is not dependent on human effort.(Titus 3: 4-5)

Each of these points is dealt with in detail in the studies that follow.

CHALLENGES from STUDY 2

 What were your ideas about God before you began this course?

 What change is there now in your thoughts about God?

 What characteristic of God mentioned in this study is most important to you in your present situation?

 What is your reaction to the facts about God in this study?

 Write down further questions on this subject you will ask your group leader or Christian friend.

ACTION

 Learn and/or write down Romans 1:20.
Find out how many stars have been seen by astronomers.

STUDY 3
GOD - A WONDERFUL PERSON

Reading: *Psalm 103*

In this song of praise we find many aspects of God's character.

v 1	He is holy.
vv 2-5	He forgives sins and cares for every area of our lives.
vv 6	He is just and will ensure justice.
vv 7-8	He is compassionate and full of love.
vv 9-12	His judgements are tempered with mercy.
vv 13-16	He has pity on our human weaknesses.
vv 17-18	His love is everlasting.
vv 19-22	He rules over the whole world.

" O God please show me what kind of person you are."

God has shown us many things about himself in his creation; his power, wisdom, goodness, love of beauty – but we need the Bible and especially Jesus Christ to tell us more.

We have seen what God is like now let us think about his character

God is **love**   John 3:16
        his very nature is love, he can never be unloving   1 John 4:10
                                                  Ps. 136:1-3

God is **holy**   Isa. 6:1-4
        absolutely without any defect or blemish   1 John 1:5

God is **righteous**   Ps. 145:17
      he is the standard for our lives   Ezra 9:15

God is **just**
      he can never be unfair – his judgements are   Gen. 18:25
      based on perfect knowledge   Rom. 2:2

God is **compassionate**
      he feels for the plight of the poor and down-trodden   Ps. 145:8-9
                                                                 Matt. 9:36

God **cares** for his people
      he watches over his people all the time   Matt. 6:25-34

God is **faithful**   Lam. 3:22-23
      he is always true to his promises   1 Thess. 5:24

God is **gracious**   Exod. 34:6
      he loves people who do not deserve it   Neh. 9:17

God is **merciful**
      he takes pity on the weak, and withholds his judgement
      from those who ask for his mercy   Luke 6:36
                                                                 1 Tim. 1:16

God is **joyful**   Neh. 8:10
      he delights in his people   Zeph. 3:17

"Thank you Lord you have not left us in the dark about yourself, you have made yourself known."

QUESTIONS ASKED ABOUT STUDY 3

In view of all the injustice in the world, and since God is in control how can he be just, as it says in Gen. 18:25?

That text is a good clue. Abraham was faced with the very problem this question poses. We can paraphrase what Abraham meant: "I do not understand what is going on, I do not understand what God is doing, but I am quite certain whatever happens God will do what is just and right".

We cannot always understand God's ways, and often our faith is tested – but in the end we will see that justice has been done.

We should remember that we see only a small part of God's ways. If we could see the whole picture we would understand. We only see the underside of the tapestry which is ugly, but the other side is beautiful.

How can a God of love command the destruction of whole nations including women and children?

Two examples of this are found in Deut. 20:16-17 and I Sam. 15:1-3. The fact that a God of love gave such commands should not make us question his love but realise that there must have been a very serious reason. God's love was exercised in two ways. First, he gave them ample time to forsake their terrible corruption. Second, he acted to save that corruption spreading to other nations – as a surgeon amputates a limb to save the body.

The evils in those nations infected the women so that they led the way in the foulest of sins, and this spread so deeply to their children there was no cure. God is love – he is also holy – he hates sin because it is offensive to him and also because it ruins people. If he did not restrain human corruption mankind would destroy itself.

How can a just God punish 'children and their children for the sin of the fathers to the third and fourth generation'? (Exod. 34:7)

We need to compare this text with God's assurances in other places that punishment for sin will apply only to the one who sins, not to someone else (Ezek. 18:1-4). The text from Exodus does not apply to eternal punishment, but to the fact that families suffer here and now because of their parents' sins and that sometimes this suffering extends in one form or another to coming generations. We see this in the history of King David (2 Sam. 12:1-14), and in the effects of drug addiction, aids and child abuse. This solemn fact should make parents take their responsibilities very seriously, but this warning from a loving God is all too often ignored.

QUESTIONS ASKED ABOUT STUDY 3

I can't believe in a God who punishes people.

We are always in difficulty when we do not submit our minds and hearts to the authority of the Bible; God is seen there to punish evildoers and his judgements are always just and based on complete knowledge. The Bible also shows us that God himself was prepared to endure the pain of seeing his only Son bear punishment due to us. One of the great comforts of the Christian message to a suffering world is the fact that God is just and that in the end justice will be done and all wrongs will be avenged. It is the God of loving justice who rules the world.

I have serious doubts about God and religion.

Many people have had such doubts taken away like Thomas (John 20:19-29). The Lord is able to convince us in ways that often surprise us. You need to be sure your doubt is genuine or if it is really a rejection of what you know to be true because you do not want your life to be changed (read John 3:19). If you sincerely want to be sure then keep on searching because the Lord has promised you will find him (Matt. 7:7-8; Rom. 10:17).

Why does God allow wars?

It is natural we should want God to stop human conflict with its gruesome consequences. But at the same time we hang on to the right of men and women to make choices and to suffer for them. If God denied us this right we would be robots and not human beings. In **Study 7** we will see why people choose violence; we must not blame God for our wrong choices. Here are some more clues:

- While God is not responsible for man's violence, he nevertheless uses wars to bring judgement on wicked nations (e.g. Nineveh – Nahum 1:14).

- God allows wars to show us what a mess we make of life without him. Wars shout out a message we still refuse to hear.

- The cause of innocent sufferers will not go unheeded. Every injustice will be vindicated in the end because God is just. God has provided a way of peace through Jesus Christ. When people are born again and trust the Lord their animosity is subdued as churches composed of Jews and Arabs (and of Irish loyalists and republicans) proves.

QUESTIONS ASKED ABOUT STUDY 3

Why does God allow human suffering?

In **Study 7** we will see that suffering in all its forms is the result of human sin and rebellion against God. This does not mean that each individual's suffering is of necessity the direct result of personal sin. Job was a very good man and yet he suffered more than most (Job 1 & 2). Nor does it mean that God is unconcerned at human pain (Isa. 63:9). Suffering leads some people to rebel against God, but true faith will enable us to believe that God has a wise purpose in his dealings with us. We may not understand this immediately but here are some clues to what his purpose might be:

- Often people are deaf to God until he makes them listen to him for their good using painful experiences to break down resistance.

- It is in suffering that we prove the strength, love and comfort of God in a deeper way than is possible without it. God may be drawing us away from a way of life that is more harmful to us than the suffering itself.

- Through suffering we learn a little of what it meant for God to give his only Son to die for people like us who do not deserve his love.

Isn't faith just a leap in the dark?

There are all kinds of faith. It can be a sort of optimism, hoping God is there but not being sure. It may be belief that God exists on the reasonable evidence of the world we live in. It is sometimes a gamble, taking a chance on Christianity and hoping it is a winner. But true faith is a gift of God himself giving us an inner certainty about him and what he says in the Bible. This faith is confirmed by the evidence of history, nature and human experience. It is not based on reason but it is by no means without reason and adequate evidence.

CHALLENGES from STUDY 3

 King David said. "My soul will boast in the LORD" (Psalm 34:2) Can you boast in God? If not, why not?

 Which of the characteristics of God in this study is the greatest comfort to you? Why?

 Is there something about God in this study that is new to you? What is it?

 Head knowledge about God is good but must lead to love for him and worship of him. Does this study affect you in this way?

 Write down further questions on this subject you will ask your group leader or Christian friend.

ACTION

 Learn and/or write down Psalm 145:8-9.   Think of specific ways in which God has been good to you — write them down.

King David said "My soul will boast in the LORD" (Psalm 34:2) Can you boast in God? If not why not?

 Which of the characteristics of God in this study is the greatest comfort to you. Why?

 Is there something about God in this study that is new to your thinking, is it?

 ...stead knowledge about God is good but must lead to love for him and worship of him. Does this study affect you in this way.

 Write down further questions on this subject you will ask your group leader or Christian friend.

 Read and/or write down Psalm 145:8-9. Think of specific ways in which God has been good to you – write them down.

STUDY 4
GOD - THREE IN ONE

Reading: *Matthew 3:13-17*

These verses refer to three persons who are God; Jesus the Son; the Spirit of God, and the Father.

vv 13-15   Up to this point Jesus has grown naturally from childhood to manhood. Now he was ready to begin his public work and his baptism was his commitment to that work.

v 16   The Spirit from God came to him to equip him for the work he came to do.

v 17   The Father's voice confirmed that Jesus Christ was no other than his Son.

The word 'Trinity' is not in the Bible, but when we take into account all the Bible says about God we conclude he is one God in three persons – Father, Son and Holy Spirit.

> " Dear God, make me willing to accept as much about yourself as you want me to know."

God first revealed himself as *one* God   Deut. 6:4
Then Jesus Christ came   John 1:14
Then the Holy Spirit was given   Acts 2:32-33

The complete revelation is summed up in these two verses

"Therefore go and make disciples of all nations, baptising them in the name of the Father and of the Son and of the Holy Spirit" (Matt. 28:19).

"May the grace of the Lord Jesus Christ, and the love of God, and the fellowship of the Holy Spirit be with you all" (2 Cor. 13:14).

The Trinity was anticipated in the Old Testament when God
referred to himself as "us"   Gen.1:26 ; Isa. 6:8

The evidence in the Bible can be stated like this

• The Father, Son and Holy Spirit are distinct persons   John 8:16;
                                                   10:30; 14:16,26.

• The Father, Son and Holy Spirit are each said to be God
    The Father   John 20:17
    The Son   Acts 20:28; Rom. 9:5
    The Holy Spirit   Acts 5:3-4

• Nevertheless there is but one God   Deut. 6:4,
                                                  John 10:30

 While God always acts as one Being, yet each of the three persons has a distinctive role

we see this

    in creation   initiated by the Father   Gen. 1:1
                         executed by the Son   John 1:3
                         completed by the Spirit   Gen. 1:2

    in prayer   when we pray to God as our heavenly Father
                         we approach him through Jesus Christ and
                         with the help of the Holy Spirit   Eph. 2:18

    in salvation   Eph. 1:3–14

    vv 3–5   *"Praise be to the God and Father of our Lord*
                         Jesus Christ, who has blessed us in the heavenly realms
                         with every spiritual blessing in Christ. For he chose
                         us in him before the creation of the world to be holy
                         and blameless in his sight. In love he predestined us to
                         be adopted as his sons through Jesus Christ, in
                         accordance with his pleasure and will."

                         Our deliverance from sin and its consequences has been planned and initiated by God the Father.

vv 6–8

*"To the praise of his glorious grace, which he has
freely given us in the One he loves. In him we have
redemption through his blood, the forgiveness of sins
in accordance with the riches of God's grace that
he lavished on us with all wisdom and understanding."*

**The first part of the plan was carried out by Jesus
Christ, God's Son, when he died on the cross.**

vv 13-14

*"And you also were included in Christ when you
heard the word of truth, the gospel of your salvation.
Having believed, you were marked in him with a seal,
the promised Holy Spirit, who is a deposit guaranteeing
our inheritance until the redemption of those who
are God's possession — to the praise of his glory."*

**The work is continued in our lives by the Holy
Spirit – his presence in our hearts is God's seal
that we belong to him.**

" O Lord, you are very great and beyond my understanding, I want
to worship you."

NOTE:

See more about the identity of:
    Jesus Christ in **Study 9**
    The Holy Spirit in **Study 12**

QUESTIONS ASKED ABOUT STUDY 4

I cannot understand the Trinity.

Try to distinguish between understanding the teaching and understanding the Being of God. None of us can understand how God can be one Being and yet three Persons, but we can understand that this is what the Bible teaches. We can accept the facts God has revealed to us in the Bible, but we must not try to apply our logic to those facts — God himself cannot be contained in logical propositions.

Do we need to accept this teaching?

All that God tells us in the Bible comes to us with his love and is good for us. As we go on in the Christian life difficult things become clearer, and things we thought were unimportant become more and more precious to us. So it will be with the teaching of the Trinity.

Some people say that a triangle is a good illustration of the Trinity.

It may help a little but God is unique and there is no illustration that can adequately explain him. But it is not surprising that his creation reflects his trinitarian being e.g.

       Time is threefold — past, present and future.
       Nature is threefold — animal, vegetable and mineral.
       Space is threefold — length, breadth and height.

Does this teaching mean there are three gods?

No. As you have seen in the study, the Bible insists that God is one. We cannot understand this mystery but we must accept what God tells us about himself, because there is no way that we could work it out for ourselves. If we could comprehend God he would not be worthy of our worship and trust.

What advantage is there in a Trinity over belief in many gods?

The gods of polytheism (belief in many gods) are fearsome, unforgiving and unable to communicate with people. Our God is awesome, but he is also forgiving and able to speak to us in Scripture by his Holy Spirit. The gods of polytheism are all on the same earthly level. In the Trinity God is above us, around us and, when we are believers, within us.

CHALLENGES from STUDY 4

 What change has this study made in your thoughts about the Trinity?

 What difference does this make to your attitude to worship?

 Write down further questions on this subject you will ask your group leader or Christian friend.

ACTION

 Learn and/or write down Matthew 28:18-20.
Find out what the "God" of Islam is like.

STUDY 5
GOD - HAS SPOKEN

Reading: *2 Timothy 3:10 – 4:5*

3:10-12   Anyone who teaches what God says in the Bible and lives consistently with that teaching must expect opposition and persecution in some form or other.

v 13   We must expect false teaching and ungodliness to increase in intensity.

vv 14-15   True teaching from the Bible can be recognised because it leads to faith in Jesus Christ for salvation which is God's pardon for our sin and acceptance with him.

v 16   The Bible is not the record of man searching for God, but of God making himself, his truth and his purposes known to us. What the Bible says God says!

vv 17 - 4:2 The Bible is completely adequate and authoritative for every aspect of our lives.

vv 3-5   Our confidence in the Bible must not be shaken by the departure of others from its teaching. Its truth does not depend on human opinion but on its origin in God himself.

" Lord, you seem to be silent, please speak clearly to me. "

God often spoke directly to people before the Scriptures were complete
Gen. 2:15-17; 15:1;
Josh. 1:1-9; Jer. 1:4-5;
1 Sam. 16:1;
Gal. 1:11-12

"In the past God spoke to our forefathers through the prophets at many times and in various ways." Heb. 1:1

God continues to speak:

through nature   Ps. 19:1; Rom. 1:19-20
through conscience   Rom. 2:15
through Scripture   Rom. 4:3;
                                            2 Peter 1:19-21
through preaching based on the Scriptures   1 Cor. 1:21; Heb. 4:12;
                                            1 Thess. 2:13-14

The authority of Scripture is rooted in Jesus Christ

he accepted the Old Testament as God's truth	Luke 16:27-31; 24:44; John 5:39-40
his own teaching is recorded in the Gospels	Luke 4:16-21; Acts 1:1-2
he revealed his truth to the apostles by his Spirit	John 16:12-15; 1 Cor. 11:23; 15:3
he is God speaking to us	John 1:1-3; Heb. 1:1-2

We must use the Bible as our final authority on all questions about our faith and our life

Isa. 8:19-20; Matt. 22:29; Acts 17:11; Acts 28:23

Jesus did	Matt. 19:1-6
Peter did	Acts 2:14-21
the early church did	Acts 15:12-21
Paul did	Acts 17:1-3

The Bible tells us what God says about our attitudes to

parents	Eph. 6:1-3
children	Prov. 22:6; Eph. 6: 4
employers	Eph. 6:5; Col. 3:33
employees	Eph. 6:9; Col. 4:1
work	Col. 3:23
husbands	Eph. 5:22-23
wives	Eph. 5:25
ourselves	Rom. 12:1-2
other people	1 Peter 2:17
the world	1 John 2:15-17
church	Rom. 12:3-8

NOTE: the Bible has much more to say on each of these subjects

" O Lord, other people seem to hear you speaking, help me to recognise your voice."

QUESTIONS ASKED ABOUT STUDY 5

How can we be sure the Bible is from God?

By taking notice of what a remarkable book it is:
a) Its amazing unity despite being written by about 30 authors over a period of about 1500 years.
b) Its profound wisdom which we could not work out for ourselves.
c) Its fulfilled prophecy. Events happened exactly as they had been predicted hundreds of years earlier (e.g. details of the birth, life, death, resurrection and glory of Jesus Christ).

By taking note of the powerful effect of its teaching:
a) In changing the lives of corrupt people.
b) In sustaining the faith of believers in very traumatic situations (e.g. martyrs).
c) In generating spiritual revivals with lasting effects on whole communities.

How did God tell the people who wrote the Bible what to say?

We do not know the exact process, all we are told is that they were 'carried along by the Holy Spirit' (2 Peter 1:21) – as a yacht is driven by the wind. However, it is clear that the Holy Spirit superintended the authors so that, using their own individual personalities, situations and experiences, they recorded without error what God intended them to say. This is why each book bears its own character and style. There were times when writers did not understand the exact meaning of what they wrote (1 Peter 1:10-12).

Isn't the Bible full of mistakes?

People who say this often have difficulty in telling us where the supposed mistakes are. Others will point to a few apparent contradictions, most of which are easily resolved with a little further study. Those that remain arise from copyists' errors and have no bearing on the teaching of Scripture. Other examples are where the Bible differs from the teaching of scientists or historians. As human knowledge has progressed the Bible has always proved to be right and there is no doubt it will continue to be vindicated.

Why are there variations between translations of the Bible?

The original Scriptures were exactly what God intended. Since then copies have been made and then copies of those copies, and so on. Then there have been translations and these in turn have been used for further translations. In the process it would be very surprising if variations did not occur but it is true to say that the differences between the existing Hebrew and Greek manuscripts are a very small proportion of the total and do not in any way affect basic Christian teaching.

QUESTIONS ASKED ABOUT STUDY 5

Some people say that Paul's letters have a different message from the teaching of Jesus.

This kind of statement can only be made on the basis of a superficial reading of the New Testament. The teaching of Jesus is supposed to be simpler and more loving than that of Paul; but the discussions between Jesus and the Jews in John, chapters 5-8 will test anyone's mental powers, and Jesus' denunciations in Matt. 23:13-36 are some of the sternest words to be found anywhere in Scripture.

On the other hand Paul in Rom. 8:38-39, 1 Cor. 13:1-7 and 1 Thess. 2:1-19 lacks nothing in both clarity and compassion. The Bible is consistent throughout and all Paul's teaching has its roots in the Old Testament and in the life and words of Jesus Christ.

Have not the Dead Sea Scrolls put a question mark over the Bible?

When the scrolls were first discovered many wild predictions were made that orthodox Christianity would suffer from their revelations. In the following fifty years an army of scholars have disagreed among themselves about the way the scrolls relate to the Bible and to the life and teaching of Jesus Christ. Generally those who began with a sceptical view of the Bible have remained so, and the faith of those who trust the Bible has not been undermined, but rather their faith has been confirmed. The contents of the scrolls are very fascinating and worthy of study and they contain nothing that proves the Bible as we have it untrustworthy.

Why do we have the sixty six books of the Bible and no more?

Jesus is the authority on all things and he confirmed the thirty nine books of the Old Testament which were the Bible of his day. He accepted them without question, quoting from them and using them as the word of God. As we have seen in the study the New Testament books also bear the marks of his authority. There are other books called the Apocrypha that are included in some Bibles but their contents are not of the same exalted character as our Bible and in some places they have ideas that are contrary to the teaching of the apostles.

The story of how the sixty six books were accepted as God's Word by the churches is a remarkable record of the Lord's supervision giving us confidence in the Bible as we have it. Ask your leader if you would like to know more about that.

CHALLENGES from STUDY 5

 Do you have difficulty in accepting the authority of the Bible, if so why?

 Are there areas of your life in which you do not submit to Scripture?

 What occasions have there been when God has spoken to you through the Scriptures?

 Write down further questions on this subject you will ask your group leader or Christian friend.

ACTION

 Learn and/or write down Hebrews 1:1-2.
Find out how many times Jesus quoted from the Old Testament.

STUDY 6
GOD - MADE US

Reading: *Psalm 8*

vv 1-2   God is to be praised because his majesty and glory are reflected in
              everything he has made.

vv 3-4   Human people are so small and insignificant compared with God
              it is surprising he takes any notice of us. But he has cared for us
              and continues to do so.

vv 5-8   In our physical limitations we are inferior to the angels, but in our
              creative abilities and in our authority over the world we are superior
              to them (compare Gen.1:26-2:7).

v9   Human people are not mere animals or machines; we are made by
              God in his image and should try to reflect him as our Creator.

In this study we consider what the Bible teaches about ourselves

> " Dear God, teach me who and what I am. If I don't know this,
> life is not worth living "

In the Bible 'man' equals men and women   Gen. 5:2

*"So God created man in his own image, in the image
of God he created him; male and female he created them." (Gen 1:27)*

We are all descendants of one couple, Adam and Eve
*"From one man he (God) made every nation of men, that they
should inhabit the whole earth." (Acts 17:26)*

Mankind is God's special creation   Ps. 139:13-16

Distinct from angels
    Angels were created by God   Ps. 148:1-6; Col. 1:16
    They already existed at creation   Job 38:4-7
    They do not have bodies like ours   Heb. 1:14

Distinct from animals   Gen. 2:19-20
    Animals do not have fellowship with God   Isa. 1:2-3
    We do

    Animals are not accountable to God   2 Peter 2:12
    We are

NOTE: This is the basis of morality – where accountability to God is denied
restraint goes (Prov. 29:18)

We are made in God's image   Gen. 1:26; James 3:9

> **NOT**   -   in our bodies – God has no body   John 4:24
>   -   'gods' as New Age teaching claims   Eccles. 5:2

> **BUT**   -   we are like God because

> > • God is a person who loves, reasons, hates,   Ps. 78:40-41;
> > and can be grieved – so are we   Isa. 1:18; 63:9;
> >   Amos 5:21; 1 John 4:7-8

> > • God is a moral being – conscious of
> > right and wrong – so are we   Ps. 25:8-9

> > • God can create things – we have a
> > creative ability   Gen. 4:17-22

> > • God has purpose – he knows what he
> > wants to do and what will satisfy him –
> > we are like that   John 5:16-17

So we should

> have self respect   Lev. 19:18; Eph. 5:29
> be impartial towards others (racism & sexism is out)   Col. 3:11; James 3:9-10

 We are both body and soul   Matt. 4:1-4; 16:26

> *" Do not be afraid of those who kill the body, but cannot
> kill the soul. Rather, be afraid of the one who can destroy
> both soul and body in hell." (Matt. 10:28)*

> Our bodies and their appetites (hunger, sex, etc) are
> not sinful they are God's gifts to us to be used,
> but they can be abused   1 Tim. 4:3-4

 **The great object of our creation is that we should
glorify God and enjoy him for ever**   Ps. 73:25-26; 1 Cor. 10:31

In the beginning humanity was perfect   Gen. 1:31
    in perfect surroundings   Gen. 2:1-9
    in perfect harmony with God   Gen. 2:15-25

> " O LORD, you created my inmost being; you knit me together in my
> mother's womb I praise you because I am fearfully and wonderfully made;
> your works are wonderful, I know that full well."   Ps. 139:13-14

QUESTIONS ASKED ABOUT STUDY 6

 Where did Cain get his wife from?

 See Gen. 5:3-5 — there was as yet no law against the inter-marrying of close relations.

 What is the answer to people who claim that science proves man came from a process of evolution and is not a special creation?

 There is evidence of some forms of evolution in the natural world, but despite confident claims and endless research there is no proof that man has evolved from animals. There are many Christians who are competent scientists and who believe that scientific research supports rather than discredits the teaching of Scripture.

 Is it important to believe that man is a special creation by God?

 It is, because
> • to deny it is to deny the clear teaching of Scripture that man arose from dust and not from a creature already existing.
>
> • to deny it is to undermine teaching in Scripture that all humans are united 'in Adam' (Rom. 5:19; 1 Cor. 15:21-22). We will see the reason for this in **Studies 7 & 12**.
>
> • the theory of evolution is used as a basis for the gradual improvement of mankind. This too is contrary to Scripture (2 Tim. 3:1-5), and to what we can see for ourselves in human history.

 Are there animals in heaven?

 It is generally assumed that death is the end for animals on the basis of such texts as Ps. 49:12; 2 Peter 2:12. But some Christians take a literal view of Isa. 11:6-8; 65:25 and think there may be some animals in the new heaven and new earth. We can be sure if we need them, the Lord will provide them!

 Doesn't the Bible make women second class citizens?

 No! The Bible sees both men and women as people with equal rights in the world and equal responsibility to God. It is true that within the church and in marriage the Bible gives women and men different roles in which men take the lead, but this is quite consistent with the total fulfilment of the talents and gifts God has given to each and of mutual benefit of the one to the other.

CHALLENGES from STUDY 6

 What change, if any, has this study made to your attitude to yourself?

 What change, if any, has this study made in your attitude to people of other races and religions?

 What should be our attitude to God as our Creator?

 Write down further questions on this subject you will ask your group leader or Christian friend.

ACTION

 Learn and/or write down Acts 17:26-27.
Make a list of the kind of people you tend to despise.

STUDY 7
SATAN – HAS SPOILED EVERYTHING

Reading: *Genesis 2:15-17; 3:1-24*

2:15-17   God was extremely generous to Adam, only one small area was denied him. God's warning about the consequences of disobedience was clear.

3:1   The serpent was Satan in disguise (Rev. 12:9); Satan was already a fallen angel (Luke 10:18) and his hostility to God is seen in his distortion of what God actually said.

vv 2-4   The distortion was quickly followed by flat contradiction of God's warning.

vv 5-6   Satan always makes the consequences of disobedience to God to be attractive.

vv 7-13   The immediate effect of Adam and Eve's sin was to destroy their harmonious relationship with God and with each other.

vv 14-19   The effect of their 'Fall' was also to be felt in the natural world.

vv 20-24   The final effect was banishment from God from which there is no return apart from God's mercy.

> " Dear Lord, this world is full of violence and pain, help me to understand why "

When God created the world – nature and humankind – all was perfect   Gen. 1:10,18,25,31

Now there is universal imperfection – this has been caused by the sin of our first parents, Adam and Eve, described in Gen. 3 – we call this 'the Fall'.

The rebellion of angels

There has been a 'Fall' among the angelic beings in which Satan led a rebellion against God   Isa. 14:12-15; Luke 10:18

A host of angels followed Satan and assist him in his hostility to the Lord and his people   2 Peter 2:4; Jude 6

Satan is also called the Devil and is a deceptive and destructive being   John 8:44

The 'Fall' of Adam and Eve
Adam and Eve were deceived – resulting in their disastrous disobedience to God   Gen. 3; 2 Cor. 11:3

The effect of the 'Fall' on humanity

"The result of one trespass was condemnation for all men." (Rom 5:18)

We are all in a sinful position – we are united to Adam by birth and consequently inherit his separation from God

Gen. 3:24;
Rom. 5:12

We have all inherited a sinful nature affecting our

Minds	Rom. 8:5-8
Hearts (affections and desires)	Gen. 6:5
Will	Rom. 7:14-24
Behaviour	Matt. 15:17-20

We all do sinful things   Rom. 3:23

A variety of words are used in the Bible to describe our wrong doing

Sin – missing the mark – set for us by	Rom 3:23
The 10 Commandments	Exod. 20:3-17
The life and teaching of Jesus Christ	John 13:15-17
Transgression – deviation – rebellion	Ps. 51:3; Eph. 2:1
Iniquity – perverse – twisted	Ps. 51:9; Isa. 59:2
Corruption – moral unsoundness	Ps. 14:1
Unrighteousness – dishonesty – injustice	1 John 1:9
Wickedness – wrong – mistaken	Isa. 55:7
Uncleaness – inner pollution	Matt. 15:10-20
Debt – moral bankruptcy	Matt. 6:12

NOTE: Each of these is used in a wider sense than its basic meaning. Together they give a comprehensive view of our lives as God sees them. Every sin is against God including wrong to others. Ps. 51:4; Rom. 8:7-8

We still bear the marks of God's image – but that image is distorted – this explains the discord, corruption and power conflicts in the world

James 4:1-3

The effect of the 'Fall' on Creation

"The creation was subjected to frustration." (Rom 8:20)

The world of nature was subjected by the judgement of God to distortion and frustration

Gen. 3:14-19,
Rom. 8:18-21

This explains cruelty among animals, earthquakes, disease in nature and ourselves etc.

This problem will be resolved by Jesus Christ at his Second coming.
(see **Study 22**)   2 Peter 3:11-13

The consequences of the 'Fall' for us

"Like the rest we were by nature objects of wrath." (Eph. 2:3)

We are under God's wrath   John 3:36; Rom. 1:18

Therefore
- we are separated from God   Isa. 59:2; Eph. 4:18

- we face eternal punishment (see **Study 22**)   Matt. 25:46

- we are spiritually dead – totally unable to do anything to save ourselves from God's condemnation   Eph. 2:1; Col. 2:13

This teaching is important because

- it helps us to understand what is happening in the world around us

- it helps us to understand ourselves

- it helps us to understand why people abuse the good things in the world

- it shows us our need of Jesus Christ

" O God, if all this is true I am in such a situation that only you can rescue me."

NOTE: All that follows in this book is about the way God completely reverses the consequences of the 'Fall'

We have a threefold need

- Pardon and reconciliation to God – because we are condemned by God

- Inner transformation – a new nature in place of the old one

- Release of us from this fallen world and the release of creation from the effects of the 'Fall'

Each of these needs is met in Jesus Christ   John 14:6

QUESTIONS ASKED ABOUT STUDY 7

 Why did God allow sin to come into the world?

 The Bible does not answer this question, so we must conclude that we are not meant to speculate. We must accept the fact of sin and face the problems it causes. The most we can say is that whatever God does or allows is never inconsistent with his character – his love, mercy, holiness, and justice.

 Since some texts in the Bible tell us that God planned the way of salvation before creation, surely the 'Fall' had to happen?

 We must always be careful when making logical conclusions from Scripture teaching, that those conclusions do not violate other teaching in the Bible. Our logic is at best imperfect because our minds are affected by the very 'Fall' we are considering. This is especially important when trying to understand God's plans and purposes. If we say the 'Fall' had to happen, we take away Adam's responsibility for what he did which is to contradict all the Bible says about Adam's responsibility and ours. So it is best not to draw such conclusions even though they seem logical to us.

 Are not all the ills of the world caused by man – why blame God for them?

 It is certainly true that the world's ills are the result of Adam's sin but it is also true to say that God carried out his threat that if Adam sinned he would die. Since then death is universal and God continues to inflict his judgements on the world because of man's continuing sin.

 If mankind is universally sinful how are some people who are not Christians so good? Is there not some good in all of us?

 Many people are outwardly good and none are as bad as it is possible for them to be. This is because of the restraints God has put into the world such as conscience in each person and governments over tribes and nations. We need to remember, however, that apparently good people can be filled with pride and covetousness which God hates and none of us is obedient to the command to 'love the Lord your God with all your heart and with all your soul and with all your mind, and with all your strength' (Mark 12:30). For this reason we read 'All of us have become like one who is unclean, and all our righteous acts are like filthy rags' (Isa. 64:6).

QUESTIONS ASKED ABOUT STUDY 7

 What would have happened if Adam and Eve had not sinned?

 This is an understandable question, but the Bible does not satisfy our curiosity. If we knew the answer this would be of no benefit to us.

 Can we really take the story of a talking serpent in Genesis 3 literally?

 If the story were not true one would have to be invented to explain the sudden break of fellowship between Adam and Eve and God, and the immediate subjection of the whole of humanity to corruption and death. But the New Testament does confirm the truth of the account (2 Cor. 11:3).

 Isn't God's judgement on the world an over reaction to a small indiscretion?

 When we doubt the fairness of any judgement we have to acknowledge that we may not be in possession of all the facts and principles involved. By the nature of the case, when we are considering God's judgements we are at a very great disadvantage. For instance, we are certainly not able to view the seriousness of sin as God does. We cannot understand his holiness and wisdom sufficiently to say that any sin is insignificant.

Nevertheless we can draw important conclusions from the fact that (as we shall see in **Study 10**) in providing for our salvation God took great care to ensure that his justice was satisfied, by punishing our sin either in us or in a substitute. Furthermore, when we remember the substitute he provided was his own dear Son, we can have no doubt of the serious view he takes of sin, or of his absolute commitment to justice.

CHALLENGES from STUDY 7

 What evidence of the 'Fall' do you see in society?

 Are you willing to accept what God says about each of us?

 Write down further questions on this subject you will ask your group leader or Christian friend.

ACTION

 Learn and/or write down Psalm 51:1-2.
Ask two or three friends seriously and honestly to tell you your faults!
Do not be cross with them!!

STUDY 8
JESUS CHRIST - HOW HE CAME

Reading: *Luke 1:26 - 2:20*

1:26-29	There would be no answer to our need if God had not taken the initiative. Mary was not sinless, but she lived a godly life.
vv 30-33	The description of the child was consistent with Old Testament predictions and Mary would immediately recognise this.
vv 34-38	The question of how a virgin could conceive is answered for ever by the words 'nothing is impossible with God'.
2:1-5	Luke is careful to set the scene in history that can be checked. Our faith is rooted in historical facts.
vv 6-7	The conception of Jesus was miraculous (without the involvement of a man) but his birth was entirely normal.
vv 8-20	The coming of Jesus was the best news this world has ever heard.

" Dear Lord, Jesus Christ came a long time ago; please help me to see what that should mean to me now. "

" Here is a trustworthy saying that deserves full acceptance: Christ Jesus came into the world to save sinners." (1 Tim. 1:15)

This is the beginning of God's answer to our problems resulting from the 'Fall'   Matt. 1:20-21

Christianity is totally dependent on Jesus Christ himself that is why he always drew attention to himself   John 15:1-5

The coming of Jesus Christ into the world was predicted in the Old Testament

He would be a prophet   Deut. 18:17-19;
                                         Acts 3:22-23

He would be a priest   Ps. 110:4;
                                         Heb. 7:20-22

He would be a king   Dan. 7:13-14;
                                         Luke 1:32-33

NOTE: 'Messiah' = Anointed One; prophets, priests and kings were appointed by the anointing with oil

Exod. 30:30; 1 Sam. 15:1; Isa. 61:1

His birth would be in very dark days	Isa. 9:1-2; Matt. 4:12-16
His birth would be in Bethlehem	Micah 5:2; Matt. 2:6
His birth would be of a virgin	Isa. 7:14; Matt. 1:22-23

NOTE: Notice how Old Testament predictions were fulfilled.

The coming of Jesus Christ into the world is explained in the New Testament

He came from a situation of glory with God the Father	2 Cor. 8:9; Phil. 2:6-8
His growth as a boy and youth was completely natural	Luke 2:39-40; 51-52
At the same time he became aware of his special relationship with God the Father	Luke 2:41-50
During thirty years of growth to manhood he pleased the Father in everything	Luke 3:21-23

" O God, thank you for sending your Son into the world. "

QUESTIONS ASKED ABOUT STUDY 8

Don't some people say that Mary was sinless?

Yes they do, but Mary herself demonstrated her awareness of sin and her need of salvation by calling God her Saviour (Luke 1:46-47).

Did Mary have other children in the normal way?

Yes. The Bible nowhere teaches that Mary was a perpetual virgin but we are told that Jesus had brothers and sisters (Matt. 13:53-56), and there is no reason why these should not have been Mary and Joseph's natural children.

How can we be sure the virgin birth actually happened?

There is no reason for us to doubt it since with God everything is possible (Luke 1:37). Luke was both a doctor and a trustworthy historian (Luke 1:1-4) who researched the matter very thoroughly. Everyone else born naturally is sinful, but Jesus was sinless (Heb. 4:14-15), the one exception out of the whole of humanity. This can only be explained by the fact that he came into the world in a different way from all the rest of us.

If Mary was sinful how was her sinful nature not conveyed to Jesus?

We do not know the exact procedure by which sinful nature is transmitted from parents to children in the normal way, so we cannot know how that procedure is by-passed. When Mary herself asked "Why?" the answer was 'The Holy Spirit will come upon you and the power of the Most High will overshadow you....' (Luke 1:35). The sinless life of Jesus can only be explained by the intervention of the Holy Spirit in some way keeping the human nature of Jesus free from corruption.

CHALLENGES from STUDY 8

 Why is it important to believe in the account of Jesus Christ's virgin conception?

 What does this teach us about God's view of our condition?

 How should this affect our worship?

 Write down further questions on this subject you will ask your group leader or Christian friend.

ACTION

 Learn and/or write down Luke 1:35.
Look up every translation you can find of Luke 2:14.

STUDY 9
JESUS CHRIST – WHO HE IS

Reading: *Matthew 16:13-21*

v 13   The disciples had lived with Jesus, they had heard his teaching, seen his miracles and his perfect character. The time had come for them to say if they knew his real identity.

v 14   The people in general rated Jesus very highly, but not highly enough.

v 15   This is still the most important question that anyone can face.

v 16   On behalf of the rest Peter gives his conclusion that this man Jesus is none other than God himself. A son is of the same order and substance as his father – he is human. When Peter says 'Son of the living God' he means that Jesus is God, as the Father is God.

v 17   The disciples had the same evidence as the rest of the people, but God had enlightened their minds.

vv 18-19   Peter is not the "rock" but this was the meaning of his name, so Jesus used this to make clear what he was saying. The rock on which the church is built is Jesus Christ who is both God and Man.

v 20   Jesus did not want popular acclaim just then, because this would hinder the many other things he had yet to do.

v 21   Now that the disciples were clear as to Jesus' identity, he could begin to show them what he came into the world to do.

> " O Lord, if I am to trust Jesus Christ I need to be sure who and what he is. "

The virgin will be with child and will give birth to a son, and they will call him "Immanuel" – which means, "God with us". (Matt. 1:23)

In order to rescue us from our plight caused by sin, God's Son took on a human nature – he became Jesus Christ – both God and Man   Phil. 2:5-8

Jesus Christ is truly human

> *"The Word became flesh and lived for a while among us". (John 1:14)*

He has a real human nature – not God pretending to be man   1 John 4:1-3

He lived – talked – thought – felt as a man | John 1:14;
Heb. 2:14; 4:15

He experienced

- tiredness | John 4:6
- temptation | Matt. 4:1
- hunger | Matt. 4:2
- thirst | John 4:7
- sorrow | John 11:35
- disappointment | Matt. 26:40
- desire for companionship | Luke 22:14-15

Jesus Christ is truly God

"In Christ all the fullness of the Deity lives in bodily form." (Col. 2:9)

He has a real divine nature – not a man pretending to be God | Col. 1:15-20

He   performed miracles | John 20:30-31
displayed miraculous knowledge | John 2:23-25
accepted worship | John 20:26-29
pardoned sins | Matt. 9:1-2
was absolutely perfect
the Father said so | Matt. 17:5
Jesus was aware of it | John 8:46
his life displayed it | 1 Peter 2:21-24
the New Testament letters declare it | 2 Cor. 5:21;
Heb. 4:15;7:26
is the judge of all | Matt. 25:31-32

He is called the Son of God
a son is not inferior to his father, they are of | Matt 1:27;16:13-17
the same nature - this is another way of saying | John 5:16-18;
that Jesus is God | Heb. 1:1-3

He is called the Word

This was understood as the wisdom of God expressed   John 1:1-3,14;
in a person – this person is said to be God and is   Col. 2:1-3
identified as Jesus Christ

We cannot explain how one person can have two natures

but   this is the only conclusion we can draw from   1 Tim. 3:16;
the evidence in the Bible   Heb. 4:15

and   this unique person meets our needs

AS MAN – he can understand our problems
    – was able to die in our place   Heb. 2:14

AS GOD – his death covered the sins
of a great number of people – his wisdom and   2 Cor. 5:18-19;
power are available to people in all ages   Heb. 13:8

NOTE: Jesus Christ requires a verdict from us.
    "What about you? Who do you say I am?" (Matt. 16:15)

He was either Mad, Bad or God

Mad   because if he is not God his claims are irrational.

Bad   because if he is not God he was a deceiver.

God   because everything about him confirms his claim to be true.

" O Lord, help me to come to the right conclusion about Jesus Christ. "

QUESTIONS ASKED ABOUT STUDY 9

Is Jesus mentioned in history apart from the New Testament?

Yes! Many times by ancient secular writers such as Josephus, Pliny the younger, Cornelius Tacitus and in the writings of Jewish rabbis.

It is said that the story of Jesus in the New Testament was invented at a later time by the church. Is this true?

No! Historians tell us there was not enough time between the events and the writings for this to happen. All four Gospels were in circulation less than 60 years after the death of Jesus so their accounts could easily have been disputed, but they were not. This claim is made by people who do not believe in miracles – especially the birth and resurrection of Jesus; it is speculation without supporting evidence. There is no reason to doubt the trustworthiness of the Gospels as accurate history. In 1977 Bishop J A T Robinson wrote a book 'Can we trust the New Testament?' (published by Mowbrays) in which he concluded that it 'can indeed be regarded still as a trustworthy guide to the words and work of Jesus the Christ'. This is interesting because Bishop Robinson was not an orthodox Christian.

Are miracles possible?

Yes! The God who made the world and subjected it to the laws with which we are familiar is perfectly able to adjust the working of those laws on a temporary or permanent basis.

Why do people say that Christianity stands or falls on the teaching that Jesus is both God and Man?

Because, if he is not who he said he is then he is not a trustworthy person, his teaching is suspect and his death will not be sufficient as a substitute for all who trust him.

QUESTIONS ASKED ABOUT STUDY 9

 How can it be true that Jesus experienced genuine human life when, for example, he was not married? Nor could he have experienced childbirth.

 Human emotions are universal and do not depend on specific circumstances. To use the examples in the question – married life and childbirth involve love, joy, fear, hope, physical pleasure and pain and much more. Jesus went through all these human feelings even though the situations were different.

 I can't understand how anyone can be both God and man.

 We do not fully understand other people, whoever they are. Each of us is unique, with a complex bodily construction, personality and temperament, and yet we can have effective relationships with one another. None of us can comprehend the unique person of Jesus Christ but we can communicate with him and trust him completely.

 Other men have claimed to be God, why should we believe Jesus any more than them?

 For a complete answer you would need to read about each of these other people to see if their lives make their claims believable. Such an investigation will show that, other than Jesus, they all betrayed imperfection in some form, failed to live up to their own ideals or were even plain frauds. The Bible says that the proof of Jesus being God is his resurrection three days after his crucifixion. (Rom. 1:4)

 In Matt. 16:17-19 didn't Jesus mean that his church would be built on Peter and that he and his successors have all authority in the church?

 No, because if this is the meaning there would be no point in the Lord's question about his own identity. A complete answer needs a detailed examination of each phrase and of the idioms and tenses used. Briefly, Jesus is using a play on words; since Peter means 'rock' so the meaning is "good, now Peter your name means 'rock' and you have just described the rock on which my church will be built."

The remaining references to authority cannot mean a super authority is given to Peter because Paul challenged him on one occasion (Gal. 2:11-13) and Paul was right!

CHALLENGES from STUDY 9

 What is your answer to Jesus' question in Matt. 16:15?

 What teaching about Jesus Christ have you found in this study that you did not know before?

 What effect will this knowledge about Jesus Christ have on your life?

 Write down further questions on this subject you will ask your group leader or Christian friend.

ACTION

 Learn and/or write down Phil. 2:5-8.
Ask two or three of your unconverted friends what they think about Jesus Christ.

STUDY 10
JESUS CHRIST – HIS DEATH

Reading: *Mark 15:1-37*

vv 1-5   The Jewish leaders twisted Jesus' claim to be a king, making him a rebel against the Roman Emperor, so they sent him for trial to Pilate, the Roman Governor.

vv 6-11   The incredible choice of a murderer instead of Jesus is explained by the 'envy' of the leaders because of Jesus' popularity.

vv 12-15   Injustice is now compounded by infamous compromise. Pilate finds Jesus blameless, yet condemns him to crucifixion and adds yet more insult by first having him flogged.

vv 16-20   Jesus could have saved himself from this humiliation (Matt. 26:53-54), but he did not, because his death was necessary for our salvation.

vv 21-23   Jesus refused the mixture because it was a drug and he would not shrink from the pain.

vv 24-25   Crucifixion was a gruesome form of execution involving the most intense pain during a long, lingering death. It was reserved for criminals.

vv 26-30   Insult was added to insult. Jesus was put on the same level as murderers, and the passers by taunted him without scruple.

vv 31-32   Little did the Jewish leaders realise the truth of what they said; since Jesus was determined to save others there was no way he was going to save himself.

vv 33-37   Our sin separates us from God and Jesus suffered this separation because he identified himself with us.

God's Visual Aid

The Lord told Moses to build a special tent
("tabernacle") where he would meet his people   Exod. 25:8-9; 29:44-46

NOTE: detailed instructions are in Exod. 25-30

The Lord revealed his presence above the ark covered by the "mercy seat" for the Holy of Holies.	Exod. 25:10-22
There was no way to God over the high white fence – representing our efforts to be not good enough.	Exod. 27:9-15
The only way was through the beautiful gate – representing Jesus Christ, the only way to God.	Exod. 27:16-18; John 10:7-10; 14:6
The way of acceptance with God was by means of a sacrifice offered on the altar representing the death of Jesus Christ.	Exod. 27:1-8; Heb. 7:26-27; 10:11-12
The worshipper placed a hand on the animal's head before it was offered to God signifying the transfer of guilt to the animal – representing our putting faith in Jesus Christ as our substitute.	Lev. 1:4; Eph. 1:7
The high priest sprinkled some of the animal's blood in the Holy of Holies – representing Jesus Christ ascending to heaven with the virtue of his sacrifice on behalf of his people.	Lev. 16:15; Heb. 9:11-14

NOTE: we shall see more of this in **Study 12**

The high priest had the names of the 12 tribes engraven on precious stones and lodged in his breast plate and on his shoulders as he went into God's presence – representing Jesus Christ now interceding for us.	Exod. 28:6-12; Heb. 7:24-25

"Dear Lord, please help me to understand the meaning of the death of Jesus Christ."

We all need to be saved from the consequences of our sin

"Jews and Gentiles alike are all under sin"(Rom. 3:9)

We saw at the end of **Study 7** that our first need as a consequence of sin is God's forgiveness – this need must be met before ever we can think of trying to live the Christian life – it is this forgiveness that the death of Christ secures for us

All of us have broken God's law and are under his judgment	Rom. 3:19-20; 5:12
The penalty of sin is death – eternal separation from God	Gen. 2:17; Ezek. 18:4; Rom. 6:23

 To save us Jesus Christ became our substitute – He died in our place

"Christ died for sins once for all, the righteous for the unrighteous, to bring you to God." (1 Peter 3:18)

Our sin and its guilt was attributed to him consequently he was punished for our sin	Isa 53:6; Rom. 4:25; 5:6,8,21

 This substitution is confirmed by terms used about Jesus' death

'For'   Gal. 2:20 – most often means "in the place of"

'Ransom'   Matt. 20:28 – this is a price paid for the release of a prisoner or hostage – we are held prisoner to God's law and Christ sets us free

'Redeemer' Eph. 1:7 – this is a price paid to buy a possession back – God redeemed his people from slavery in Egypt by means of the blood of a slain lamb (Exod. 12:1-11; John 1:29) – Jesus was the fulfilment of all the Old Testament sacrifices

'Atonement' Rom. 3:25 – in Old Testament worship the high priest made atonement (a covering) for the people by taking the blood of a sacrificed animal into God's presence (Lev. 16:15-16)

'Propitiation' Rom. 3:25 AV and NKJV – ('sacrifice of atonement.' NIV) – "The one who would turn aside his wrath taking away sin." (NIV margin)

The substitution of Jesus Christ in our place is confirmed by three other words used of him:

'Guarantee' Heb. 7:22 – our Lord is the guarantee that all the promised blessings of pardon, peace and everlasting life will be ours – a guarantor takes the place of those being helped

'Intercessor' Heb. 7:25 and **'Mediator'** 1 Tim. 2:5 – our Lord mediates for us in God's presence presenting the value of his life and death to maintain our release from wrath

The death of Jesus Christ secures for us:

Reconciliation – to God .... 2 Cor. 5:18-19

Forgiveness .... Eph. 1:7

Justification – treated by God as though we had not sinned (see **Study 14**) .... Luke 18:9-14; Rom. 3:24; 5:1

Righteousness – the perfect obedience of Christ in his life and death, credited (imputed) to us and giving us access into God's presence .... Jer. 23:6; Rom. 1:16-17; Phil. 3:7-9

These benefits are received through faith – believing or trusting in Jesus Christ and his death for us .... John 5:24; Rom. 4:4-5; Eph. 2:8-9

The death of Jesus Christ was not an accident, but was planned by God for our salvation

John 10:14-15;
Acts 2:23;
Eph. 1:3-6;
1 Peter 1:18-20

We also learn from the death of Jesus Christ

the amazing love of God for undeserving people

John 3:16;
Rom. 5:8

the amazing love of Jesus to give himself
as a sacrifice for us

John 10:11; 13:1

an example to give ourselves willingly for the
benefit of others

John 15:9-13;
1 John 4:9-11

" O Lord, thank you for coming and giving your life for sinful people like me. "

QUESTIONS ASKED ABOUT STUDY 10

How can something that happened nearly 2000 years ago be any help to us now?

This is why it was necessary for us to discover who Jesus is before considering his death. If he is merely human there would be no virtue in his death beyond himself. But as the sinless God-Man, his death has infinite value and is not limited by time.

How can the death of one man be beneficial in any way for many other people?

As with our answer to the first question, this one is answered by the fact that Jesus Christ is both God and Man. This gives his death an infinite value – it is adequate to cover the needs of people without number who have trusted, do trust and will yet trust in him.

How were people saved who lived before the coming of Jesus Christ?

Salvation is always and only through faith in the Lord Jesus Christ. People in Old Testament days were saved on the basis of what Jesus would do for them. Their animal sacrifices, offered in obedience to God's command and accompanied by faith in God's promised mercy, pointed on to the death of Jesus Christ. He 'offered for all time one sacrifice for sins'. (Heb. 10:12)

Why do some Christian teachers reject the idea of Jesus dying as a substitute? They argue that God forgives freely as did the father in the story Jesus told in Luke 15:11-27, and that the death of Jesus is simply a wonderful proof that God loves us and is willing to forgive us.

This is a very serious rejection of the plain teaching of the Bible.
Such teachers usually do not take the Bible as completely trustworthy. They take the liberty of agreeing with some parts and disagreeing with others.
It is clear that Old Testament worship, in which animals were sacrificed in the place of people, prepared the way for New Testament teaching of substitution. This is one of the many strands that runs through the whole of the Bible and links it together.
If no penalty was paid for us then we will have to pay our own. If this were not so then God's justice would be violated – he must punish sin either in the sinner or in the substitute he has provided. Those who reject this teaching usually believe, nevertheless, that one day all the injustice in the world will be avenged – but if God compromises his justice for our salvation, there is no guarantee of ultimate justice in the world, and suffering people are left without hope.

CHALLENGES *from* STUDY 10

 What is your response to the death of Jesus Christ in the place of sinful people?

 Try to put Rom. 5:8 into your own words.

 Why do you think it is necessary for us to be reconciled to God before we can start to live in a way that pleases him?

 Write down further questions on this subject you will ask your group leader or Christian friend.

ACTION

 Learn and/or write down Isa. 53:6.
Sketch each item in the Tabernacle (Exod. 37) and try to work out its significance.

STUDY 11
JESUS CHRIST – HIS RESURRECTION

Reading: *John 19:31-20:9*

19:31-37   Jesus certainly died. What happened later was not reviving from a swoon but resurrection from death.

vv:38-42   This burial treatment resulted in the body being encased in such a way that would have been impossible for him to wake up and disrobe himself.

20:1-2   The disciples did not believe Jesus' predictions that he would rise again (Matt. 16:21), so his absence from the tomb took them completely by surprise. The stone was not removed to allow Jesus to escape (Matt. 28:2) because that was not necessary. It's removal simply exposed the emptiness within.

vv:3-9   The second disciple was most probably the apostle John. He believed a miracle had taken place when he saw the evidence that the body of Jesus had withdrawn from the clothes leaving them untouched.

> " Lord, my unbelief is being challenged, help me to be honest with the Bible and myself. "

Jesus predicted that he would 'rise again'   Matt. 17:22-23

The first preachers of the Gospel, the apostles, boldly   Acts 2:32; 4:2;
taught that Jesus Christ had come to life again   17:18

Resurrection is **NOT** the same as

    Resuscitation – some say Jesus swooned and then   John 19:33
        revived in the cool of the tomb – but he   Acts 2:24
        actually died – Roman soldiers would   1 Cor. 15:3-4
        not make a mistake

    Re-incarnation – this involves a constant sequence
        of deaths – but Jesus died once and for all   Heb. 9:28; 10:12

        Re-incarnation also involves a radical change in
        form – but Jesus was God/Man while on earth
        and he is still God/Man   1 Tim. 2:5

    Inspiration – it is true that Jesus lives on in his words
        recorded in the Bible and reflected in his disciples –
        but resurrection means he is alive and actively
        working for us and with us   Heb. 7:23-25

The resurrection of Jesus is vital for our Christian faith and personal experience

"If Christ has not been raised, our preaching is useless and so is your faith." (1 Cor. 15:14)

It demonstrated the power of God	1 Cor. 6:14; Eph. 1:18-21
It confirmed Jesus to be the Son of God	Rom. 1:4
It confirmed predictions made in the Old Testament and by Jesus himself	Luke 24:25-27, 44-46 1 Cor. 15:3-4
It was God's approval and acceptance of Jesus' life and death	Rom. 4:25; 1 Cor. 15:17

NOTE: this answers the question "How can I know God has accepted Christ's sacrifice on my behalf?"

It was a victory over Satan and his forces	Col. 2:15
It defeated the power of death	1 Cor. 15:20-22; 2 Tim. 1:10
It means that Jesus is alive today to be with his people	Matt. 28:20; Acts 9:1-6
It anticipates his return	John 14:1-3
It is the forerunner of our resurrection	Rom. 8:11
It provides the pattern of our resurrection	Phil. 3:21
It anticipates the day of judgement	Acts 17:31
It is the means by which we receive new life	Eph. 2:1-5

"If only for this life we have hope in Christ, we are to be pitied more than all men. But Christ has indeed been raised from the dead." (1 Cor. 15:19-20)

"Jesus Christ, please make yourself real to me."

QUESTIONS ASKED ABOUT STUDY 11

Can we trust the story in the Gospels?

Refer back to the answer to a similar question in **Study 9.**

What is the answer to those who say Jesus did not really die but swooned and then revived in the cool of the tomb?

It is most unlikely the soldiers who crucified Jesus were deceived. Crucified people didn't swoon — they died. Joseph and Nicodemus would not have applied the ointments and linen strips to Jesus if they had not been sure he was dead. (John 19:38-42)

How do we answer those who say that the body was stolen by the disciples while the guard soldiers slept?

It is incredible that all four soldiers whose lives depended on keeping the tomb secure could have slept while a very large boulder was being rolled away. Some sleep!!
The bribing of the soldiers was surely an admission of the facts by the authorities (Matt. 28:11-15). These authorities had every incentive to ransack the city to find the body, but they never produced it.

Some people say that the disciples suffered from hallucinations and only imagined they saw Jesus alive after his death.

It is unbelievable that every one of those who claimed to see Jesus was suffering in this way. The variety of people, times and situations is such as to make this idea not worth a second thought. Furthermore, people who argue in this way have to explain the amazing change in the disciples from fearful crest-fallen cowards to bold outspoken witnesses most (possibly all) of whom suffered violent martyrdom for their faith.

QUESTIONS ASKED ABOUT STUDY 11

What happened to Jesus between his death and his resurrection?

The only thing we can be sure about is that his body remained in the tomb until it came to life again. As to what happened to our Lord's spirit, there are a number of texts that appear to have a bearing on this but there is no clear agreement as to how they should be understood. (Luke 23:43; Eph. 4:9-10; 1 Peter 3:18-19).

What is the difference between Jesus' resurrection and his miraculous raising of dead people?

The accounts of these miracles show that those raised did not go immediately into God's presence but returned to natural life on earth (Luke 7:11-17; 8:49-56; John 11:17-44). Later they died and await the final resurrection of all believers. By contrast Jesus did not return to a normal earthly life but appeared already in his resurrection body. Those were resuscitations, our Lord's was resurrection.

What kind of body did Jesus have?

We will deal with this question in **Study 22, question 4.**

Why is it difficult to discover the exact order of events surrounding Jesus' resurrection?

We can be sure that our all-wise heavenly Father has given us the Scriptures in the form that are best suited to our needs. The writers of the Gospels did their work without consulting each other; this accounts for differences in the details of what they recorded, but the Holy Spirit supervised them so that there are no contradictions.

One reason for this arrangement may be that those who want to oppose the gospel are robbed of the possible accusation that the writers conspired to make up the stories. A forger would have been very unlikely to leave the documents as they are without attempting some harmonisation and ironing out apparent differences.

The result is four portraits of Jesus, viewed from four different angles for four distinct purposes for which we should be very grateful.

CHALLENGES from STUDY 11

 Do you think it is possible to be a Christian without believing in the resurrection?

 Are you afraid to die? Give reasons for your answer.

 What hindrances do you have, if any, to complete belief in the resurrection of Jesus Christ?

 Write down further questions on this subject you will ask your group leader or Christian friend.

ACTION

 Learn and/or write down 1 Corinthians 15:17-20.
Ask as many Christians as you can what the resurrection of Jesus means to them.

Do you think it is possible to be a Christian without believing in the resurrection?

 Are you afraid to die? Give reasons for your answer.

 What hindrances do you have, if any, to complete belief in the resurrection of Jesus Christ?

 If you have further questions on this subject you will ask your group leader or Christian friend.

 Learn and/or write down 1 Corinthians 15:17-20. Ask someone (a) Christian(s) to tell you what the resurrection of Jesus means to them.

STUDY 12
JESUS CHRIST – HIS ASCENSION

Reading: *Hebrews 10: 11-18*

v.11   Old Testament sacrifices were offered regularly and repeatedly
            (see Exod. 29:38-41). God accepted them, not because they had value
            in themselves, but because they foreshadowed the death of Jesus Christ.

v.12   Since Jesus Christ came he is the only one entitled to be a priest.
            He is our great high priest (Heb. 4:14). His sacrifice was sufficient to
            cover all the sins of all his people for ever. After his death and
            resurrection he ascended to God's presence where he "sat down"
            indicating that his work for our salvation was complete.

v.13   Among other things our Lord's presence in heaven is the guarantee
            that his enemies, and ours, will be defeated. His "waiting" is not
            inactive; he is working toward his final victory.

v.14   Jesus Christ has completely satisfied all that was necessary for our
            salvation and we are accepted in him as though we were already perfect.

vv 15-16   Jesus' ascension makes it possible for him to send the Holy Spirit who
            fulfils that part of the New Covenant (Jer. 31:31-34) that promises
            such a change of heart that people will love God's laws.

vv 17-18   The presence of Jesus Christ at the Father's side ensures that the value of
            his sacrifice for sins will never be lost but will answer for us for all time.

> " O Lord, I have not thought much about this before, help me to
> see what it should mean to me. "

Forty days after his resurrection Jesus Christ   Luke 24:50-51;
went back to his Father from whom he came   John 17:4-5;
                                                            Acts 1:1-3;9-12

From there he gave the Holy Spirit on the day of Pentecost.   John 7:37-39;
                                                            Acts 2:1-12, 32-36

NOTE: The Holy Spirit is a divine person who
                    gives spiritual life   John 6:63
                    convinces of sinfulness   John 16:7-8
                    teaches   John 16:12-13
                    leads to Jesus Christ   John 16:14-15

There he is continuing to work as our prophet, priest and king

NOTE: These offices in the Old Testament foreshadowed their
perfection in Jesus Christ

as the true **Prophet,** Jesus Christ

continues to speak through the Scriptures	Rom. 10:17; Col. 3:16
continues to speak through the Holy Spirit	John 16:7-11; 1 Thess. 1:5
continues to speak through his people	Acts 8:4; Eph. 4:7-13

*"He was a prophet, powerful in word and deed before
God and all the people". (Luke 24:19)*

as the great **High Priest,** Jesus Christ

continues to guarantee our standing with God	Rom. 8:33-34; 1 John 2:1-2
continues to meet all our need	Heb. 4:14-16
continues as our representative	Col. 3:1-3

• By faith we are united to Christ

• No longer "in Adam" but "in Him" (1 Cor. 15:22; Eph. 1:3)

• Our prayers are accepted through Him. (Eph. 2:18; 1 Tim. 2:5)

continues as our forerunner	John 14:1-3
• where he is we will surely follow him	Heb. 6:20

continues as our surety   John 17:24
   • the guarantee that we will enter heaven too   Heb. 7:22

continues to ensure our complete salvation   Heb. 7:23-25

"Such a high priest meets our need — one who is holy, blameless,
pure, set apart from sinners, exalted above the heavens". (Heb. 7:26)

as **King,** Jesus Christ

continues to rule over all things for the   John 17:2;
benefit of his people   1 Cor. 15:25-26;
                                               Rev. 19:16

continues to rule over his church   Matt. 16:16-19;
                                               Eph. 1:22-23

continues to direct the extending of his kingdom   Matt. 28:16-20

continues to work in human hearts by his Holy Spirit   Rom. 8:9

"The kingdom of the world has become the kingdom of our
Lord and of his Christ, and he will reign for ever and ever." (Rev. 11:15)

" Father thank you for being willing to accept sinful people through Jesus Christ your Son. "

QUESTIONS ASKED ABOUT STUDY 12

If God is everywhere how can we talk about Jesus going up to him?

This side of heaven there are many things about God we cannot understand, but he lovingly helps us by using images familiar to us to reveal himself and describe his actions. God is certainly everywhere; he is also superior to anything on earth. We speak of "going up" to someone who is actually standing on the same level when we mean we are approaching a superior. Jesus is equal with God, but so far as we are concerned he returned to the one who is above all.

The world does not seem to be under the Lord's control!

This is true, but it is also consistent with the way the Lord always works; when everything appears to have been out of control we suddenly realise he has been over-ruling what has happened to fit his perfect plan. For example, in the years before Jesus came the first time it would have been very difficult to see how God was at work preparing the world for that event, but now we can see that he was working step by step to fulfil his purpose. The same is true today; despite appearances, the Lord is controlling all that happens until the return of Jesus Christ.

CHALLENGES from STUDY 12

 What is there in this study you did not know or understand before?

 Does it help you to know that Jesus Christ is now in the Father's presence? If so, how?

 How do you think Jesus Christ directs his people today?

 Write down further questions on this subject you will ask your group leader or Christian friend.

ACTION

 Learn and/or write down Acts 1:8-9.
Find out from a missionary how the Lord directed him or her to their work.

STUDY 13
THE HOLY SPIRIT – COMES TO US

NOTE: at the end of **Study 7** we noted our threefold need as a result of the 'Fall' – pardon - inner transformation and release from the present evil world

PARDON   in **Studies 8–12** we saw how Jesus Christ has provided for God to forgive us

INNER TRANSFORMATION   in **Studies 13–20** we will see how the Holy Spirit works this change in us

RELEASE   this is the subject of **Studies 21–22**

Reading: *John 3:1-16*

v.1   Nicodemus was a very religious man that taught others from the Old Testament.

v.2   He had reached the conclusion that Jesus came from God but that was not enough to put him right with God.

vv 3-4   When Jesus told him he must be born again Nicodemus thought he meant some kind of physical re-birth.

vv 5-8   Jesus made clear that the new birth was not physical but spiritual and entirely the Holy Spirit's work.
"water" = physical birth
"spirit" = The Holy Spirit

vv 9-16   We know we are born again when we are able to believe in Jesus Christ and to rely on him alone for salvation from sin and all its consequences.

> " Lord, re-birth sounds very peculiar: please show me what it means. "

This new spiritual life is described as

rebirth   Titus 3:3-8 (AV "regeneration")
new creation   2 Cor. 5:17; Eph. 2:10
being made alive   Eph. 2:5; 1 John 5:11-12
baptism in the Spirit   Matt. 3:11; 1 Cor. 12:13

Because of the 'Fall' we are all naturally

spiritually dead – without real desire   Rom. 8:5-8;
for God or ability to please him   Eph. 2:1-3

When we are born again all this is reversed

we are given **repentance & faith**	Acts 11:18;
"Turn to God in repentance and	Eph. 2:1-8
have faith in our Lord Jesus."(Acts 20:21)	

Repentance is a change of mind about God and	Ps. 51:1-4
about ourselves - accompanied by	
resolve to obey God and please	I Thess. 1:8-10
him - relying on his help	

"Seek the Lord while he may be found: call on him while he is near.
Let the wicked forsake his way and the evil man his thoughts. Let him turn
to the LORD, and he will have mercy on him, and to our God, for he will
freely pardon." (Isa. 55:6-7)

Faith	is believing what God says and trusting	
	in Jesus Christ for salvation from sin	
	and all its consequences	John 3:16

Faith	is more than believing what the Bible	
	teaches - it is positive - conscious	Ezek. 33:30-32;
	reliance on Jesus Christ.	Mark 7:5-7

Faith	is the opposite to "works" - works are	
	anything we do; however good such	Rom. 4:4-5;
	things are - we are saved by faith only.	Phil. 3:3-8

 We can know we are born again if we have been given repentance and faith.

 We are not to ask if we are born again - we are to do what he says

He tells us to

seek Him	Matt. 7:7-8;
	Rom. 10:13
repent	Acts 17:30
trust in Him	John 5:24

encouraged by

his love	John 3:16
his mercy	1 Tim. 1:15-16
his willingness to receive us	John 6:37
his promises	Isa. 55:6-7

**We can know we are born again if we have the signs of life in us –
signs of physical life illustrate signs of spiritual life**

Hunger and thirst - we have a strong desire	Job 23.12
to know more of Jesus Christ and	Matt. 5:6
his teaching and to be like him	1 Peter 2:2-3

Crying and speaking - we cry to God as our Father	Ps. 32:6; 40:1
and learn how to speak to him in prayer	Rom. 8:15

Feelings of pain and pleasure - we hate sin	Ps. 16:11; 34:8
and grieve over its effects in ourselves	Ps. 119:163
and the world - we enjoy learning about	Gal. 5:22-23
God - all he is and all he is doing	Phil. 3:18

Desire for companionship - we want to spend	
time with the Lord and enjoy	1 John 1:3-4; 3:14
fellowship with him and his people	

**The new birth begins a process of overcoming sin
and becoming like Jesus Christ**   1 Thess. 5:23-24

> *"Being confident of this, that he who began a good work in
> you will carry it on to completion until the day of Christ Jesus." (Phil. 1:6)*

NOTE: If we are born again God is now our Father

" Dear Lord, help me to receive this new life and have a new beginning. "

QUESTIONS ASKED ABOUT STUDY 13

Why does the Spirit work in some people's lives and not others?

This is entirely in the will, purpose and love of God. The reason is not to be found in anything we are, have done or may promise to do. If the Spirit did not begin his work in us we would never be saved.

If it is the Spirit's work alone does this mean there is nothing we can do?

There is nothing we can do until we are born again; but as in natural birth the proof of life is breathing, hunger, movement, in the same way a person who is born again begins to pray, to hunger for spiritual food, and to explore the new life. A baby does not ask 'I wonder if I am born?' but does the things that come most naturally. If we are tempted to ask such a question it is most probably a proof that we are born again.

How can we tell the difference between a mere head knowledge and the evidence of spiritual life?

A mere head knowledge does not result in a commitment of life to Jesus Christ, implacable opposition to sin in all its forms, regular communion with God, love for God's people and a desire for holiness. Some people hesitate to confess Christ openly for fear they are motivated only by head knowledge.
The fact that they are anxious about this in all probability means they are born again and should immediately declare their faith openly.

Some people teach that the new birth comes through baptism. Is this true?

This is called 'baptismal regeneration' and arises from a mis-understanding of such texts as Mark 16:16; John 3:5; Titus 3:5-7. Regeneration is likened to washing because, as Paul tells us in Eph. 5:26 it is the cleansing application of the Word of God to our hearts by the Holy Spirit, not by water baptism. Also baptism and salvation are closely linked in Scripture because in New Testament times those who came to faith in Christ were immediately baptised, not in order to be saved but because they were saved. Close attention to John 1:12-13 and Eph. 2:1-10 will be sufficient to prove that regeneration is the direct work of the Holy Spirit in us without human intervention of any kind.

QUESTIONS ASKED ABOUT STUDY 13

Natural birth is an instantaneous event so why do some people go through long struggles in the process of becoming Christians?

Just as there is a time span between conception and physical birth, so there often is, indeed most often, a period after the Spirit begins his work in us during which we are gradually brought to sufficient understanding of the Bible and ourselves to repent and believe. Sometimes this is a period of painful inner conflict.

Were my church-going and prayers of no value at all?

They were of no value if you thought of them as a means to earn God's favour or forgiveness; remember the words of Isa. 64:6 'All of us have become like one who is unclean, and all our righteous acts are like filthy rags'. But they were very valuable as means through which you could learn about God and the way he freely forgives us.

Do we have to go through crisis experiences like painful pangs of conscience or extra-ordinary joyful feelings before we can be sure we are Christians?

No! The Lord has many ways of breaking into our minds and hearts. Some people seem to have very mild emotions, others go through agonies or tremendous feelings of elation (sometimes both). Paul had a most dramatic experience (Acts 9:1-19) but he never insisted that the same should happen to other people. The essential thing is that we have learned to hate sin and its consequences and to love Jesus Christ and holy living, no matter how we have been led. However, it is not unusual for those, whose conversion was comparatively undramatic to have crisis experiences later in their Christian life.

Must I be able to say the moment when I was born again?

No! Some people can do this but for many of us the process was so gradual that there is no precise moment we can point to. The important thing is that at this moment we are trusting Jesus Christ for God's pardon and are trying to follow him. However, one of the great benefits of believers' Baptism (see **Study 22**) is that it provides us with a date of commitment to the Lord no matter how he has led us up to then.

QUESTIONS ASKED ABOUT STUDY 13

 I am afraid I may have committed the unpardonable sin.

 This sin is mentioned by Jesus in Matt. 12:31-32. Since you are worried about it you can be sure you are not guilty of it because its very essence is implacable hardness. It refers to an opposition to Jesus Christ that is so perverse as to attribute his work to the devil. Such hardness does not have guilty feelings like yours.

 I am not sure if I have repented enough.

 You most certainly have not repented enough because none of us do. We can never realise as much as we should how much God hates our sin. Be encouraged because the very self despair in what you say is the very attitude of heart God accepts. (Ps. 51:17; Isa. 66:2)

CHALLENGES from STUDY 13

 What changes have there been in your thinking and ambitions?

 What signs do you see in yourself of new spiritual life?

 Write down further questions on this subject you will ask your group leader or Christian friend.

ACTION

 Learn and/or write down Titus 3:4-6.
Ask the most recent convert you know how he or she became a Christian.

STUDY 14
THE HOLY SPIRIT – BEGINS HIS WORK

Reading: Romans 3:19-26

vv 19-20   By 'the law' Paul means anything we do to try to please God and earn his pardon, no matter whether this is by religious observances, good deeds, respectability or any other way. But law can only show us how sinful we are and how imperfect and unacceptable are our best efforts. So, by the law we are not pardoned but condemned.

vv 21-22   The only way for us to be acceptable to God is that the perfection ("righteousness") of Christ is credited to us. This means his absolute obedience in life and death are accepted by God for us. This is an altogether different way from law keeping, and it is clearly taught in the Old Testament (Rom. 4:1-3); it is received by faith alone.

vv 23-24   Faith in Christ and what he has done for sinners is the only way for all because all are equally undeserving.

vv 25-26   God would be perfectly just to punish our sins immediately, but mercifully he has not done so. This does not mean he is no longer just. He has punished our sins already in the death of Jesus Christ, therefore, he is both just and the one who justifies (accepts as guiltless) those who trust in Jesus.

> " O God, I need to be sure that when I die I will not be condemned. "

Before we begin to live the Christian life we need to be sure we are Christians - reconciled to God

We must be sure we are reconciled to God before we can   Rom. 5:11;
    begin seeking to overcome sin and live to please him.   6:17-18

"Therefore, I urge you, brothers, in view of God's mercy, to offer your bodies as living sacrifices, holy and pleasing to God." (Rom. 12:1)

If we try to reverse this order we are

      • putting the cart before the horse

      • trying to use a broken limb before it is mended

      • trying to pay our way before past accounts have been settled

STUDY 14 Continued

 The two parts of this process are called Justification and Sanctification

Justification

When the Holy Spirit gives us faith to trust in Jesus
Christ for deliverance from sin and its consequences
we are justified   Rom. 5:1

Justified means that though we are rightly declared
guilty we are nevertheless pardoned and declared
acceptable to God as though we had never sinned   Rom. 4:4-5

Justified also means we are accepted by God just as
though we had always perfectly kept his law   Rom. 3:21-22

Sanctification

Justification is once for all - sanctification begins
immediately and is the process by which we   Rom. 6:11-14;
overcome sin and are prepared for everlasting glory   Rom. 8:28-30

 Justification and sanctification must never be separated

no sanctification without justification

no justification without sanctification

both depend on our union with Christ through faith   Gal. 2:20

Justification has to do with our position before
God not our inward condition   Rom. 5:1-2

Sanctification has to do with our inward condition
not with our position before God.

Justification is based on what Christ has done for us
and is received by faith only

Sanctification is what the Holy Spirit does within us
enabling us to strive for perfection

*"For it is by grace you have been saved, through faith - and this not from yourselves, it is the
gift of God - not by works, so that no-one can boast. For we are God's workmanship, created in
Christ Jesus to do good works, which God prepared in advance for us to do." (Eph. 2:8-10)*

*"May God himself, the God of peace, sanctify you through and through. May your whole spirit,
soul and body be kept blameless at the coming of our Lord Jesus Christ. The one who calls you
is faithful and he will do it." (1 Thess. 5:23-24)*

 " Dear Lord, lead me to know that my sins are forgiven and give me
your strength to live for you. "

QUESTIONS ASKED ABOUT STUDY 14

If we are justified by faith only will this lead to carelessness about sin?

No! Paul deals with this question in Rom. 6:1-4. His argument is that faith unites us to Jesus Christ, not only in his death, but also his resurrection, and the two are inseparable. We cannot trust Jesus' death for our salvation without at the same time receiving his resurrection power to live a new life.

What happens if we sin after we are converted? Does this cancel our justification and bring us under God's judgement again?

By no means! If a child grieves his or her father this will spoil their relationship until the matter is put right but it cannot alter the position of the child. In the same way sin will spoil our relationship with our heavenly Father but no matter what happens he is still our Father. John deals with this in 1 John 1:8 - 2:2.

Doesn't the Bible say that faith without works is dead?

Yes, in James 2:14-17. At first sight it may look as though James is contradicting Paul's teaching of justification by faith only but this is not so. James is warning us that the proof that our faith is genuine is that it leads to good deeds and holy living. There is always the danger that our faith is merely head knowledge and in verse 19 James says that even the demons have got that! We are justified by faith without works or deeds of any kind, but the same faith that trusts God for his mercy, also trusts him for his enabling to live to please him.

None of us reaches perfection in this life, does this mean the Holy Spirit has failed?

No! The Lord has not promised we will be perfect before we die. In God's sight we are already perfect because we are united by faith to Jesus Christ and we are accepted in him (1 Cor. 6:9-11). At the same time the Holy Spirit leads us toward perfection; if this is not so we must examine ourselves to see if we are really true Christians. It would seem from 1 John 3:1-3 that no matter what our exact state when we die, we will then be transformed to be like Jesus.

I have been told not to trust my feelings. What does this mean?

When we are converted we may have all kinds of feelings of shame, regrets, love, joy, elation and many more. Our conversion would be a sham if we had no feelings. But we must not say "Because I had these feelings I must be saved" or "Because I have not had these feelings I cannot be saved". Our salvation rests on what Jesus Christ has done for us not on our feelings. We may have a full range of feelings but this is no proof that they arise from true spiritual experience.

What must I give up as a Christian?

Give up anything you discover is offensive to God, anything which is a hindrance to your own spiritual life or to the growth of others, or anything that makes it difficult for you to serve the Lord with your whole heart. (Matt. 16:24-26)

CHALLENGES from STUDY 14

 What have you found difficult to understand in this study?

 Are you ready to renounce all your own efforts and trust in Christ alone for acceptance with God?

 Could you now tell someone you are a Christian and what this means to you? What would you say?

 Write down further questions on this subject you will ask your group leader or Christian friend.

ACTION

 Learn and/or write down Eph 2:8-10.
Ask a believer you respect how he or she overcomes one particular difficulty in the Christian life.

STUDY 15
THE HOLY SPIRIT – WORKS IN US

Reading: *2 Peter 1:1-11*

vv 1-2   Peter assures the Christian believers that there are more than sufficient resources available for them in Jesus Christ.

v 3   Those resources are all they need to live the Christian life and to be the kind of people God wanted them to be.

v 4   Among those resources are God's "great and precious promises" that assure us of his determination to transform our lives and make us fit for his holy presence.

vv 5-7   Far from these promises making us careless about our own endeavours to grow in godliness, we are to "make every effort" to see that they are fulfilled in us.

vv 8-9   If we do this our lives will be useful to the Lord, but if we do not strive in this way it may mean we are not Christians at all, or that we have forgotten why the Lord saved us.

vv 10-11   The proof that we have been chosen by God and will be received into glory is that we are persevering in holy living.

> " O God, if I become Christian I want to be a true one. "

The same Holy Spirit who has shown us our spiritual need and led us to repentance and faith has taken up residence in us

This is Christ living in us by the Holy Spirit   Rom. 8:9;
                                                                                       Gal. 2:20; Col. 1:27

This residence of the Spirit is like

A Seal	that proves we belong to God	Eph. 1:13
A Deposit	that guarantees the fuller amount later	Eph. 1:14; 4:30
A Firstfruit	that is a sample or foretaste of more to come	Rom. 8:11, 23

The Christian life is a process of

Trusting	in the promises of God, and the work of His Spirit in us, and	Phil. 2:12-13 Prov. 3:5-6
Trying	hard to be what God promises we will be	2 Tim. 2:19; 1 Peter 4:7-11; 1 John 3:1-3

If we trust without trying we are deceiving ourselves: if we try without trusting our efforts will fail.

Trusting	we trust the Lord for everything	2 Cor. 5:7; 1 Thess. 5:24; 2 Tim. 1:12
	for example we trust Jesus as our	
	Shepherd	John 10:27-30
	Vine (source of life)	John 15:1-5
	Teacher and Lord	John 13:13
	Intercessor	Heb. 7:25
	we trust in the promises that we are secure in Christ and will go on with him	Phil. 1:6; Col. 3:4; 1 Peter 1:3-6; Jude 24-25
Trying	Our trying must be in the Lord's strength and not our own	Phil. 4:13

The means we must use are

PRAYER	Luke 18:1; 1 Thess. 5:17

There are many kinds of prayer (Eph. 6:18)

Emergency	Neh. 2:4
Praise	Ps. 71:14
Worship	Ps. 95:6
Thankfulness	Ps. 100:4
Fellowship	1 John 1:3
Self Giving	Rom. 12:1
For Others	Eph. 6:19
For Ourselves	
for help	Ps. 18:6
for guidance	Ps. 25:4-5
for pardon	Ps. 25:11
for comfort	Ps. 119:76

BIBLE READING   Ps. 1:1-3

There are different ways of using the Bible

For Information	Josh. 1:7-8
For Study	Ezra 7:10
For Meditation	Ps. 119:15
For Help	2 Tim. 3:16-17

OBEDIENCE   John 14:15

We are not saved by obedience but for obedience

To the laws of God	1 Peter 1:14-16
To the example of Christ	1 Peter 2:21-23
To the apostles' teaching	Acts 2:42

CHURCH LIFE	Heb. 10:24-25
SPIRITUAL THINKING	Rom. 8:5-8; 12:1-2;
	Phil. 4:8

OPEN WITNESS

in Believers Baptism	Acts 2:40-41
in personal testimony	Luke 8:38-39
in Christian service	Gal. 5:13-14

" Dear Lord, this is a completely new kind of life; help me to follow it . "

How can I maintain confidence in my being justified by faith?

Faith is strengthened by applying Scripture to our mind with the help of the Holy Spirit. We need constantly to be refreshing our minds with the wonder of the gospel and the promises of God.

How can I keep my mind pure?

This is difficult if we have any kind of contact with unbelieving people or with the media. It is important for us to take positive steps to reduce our exposure to impurity (Job 31:1; Matt. 5:27-30) especially those influences that we know we are vulnerable to. But if we try to cut ourselves off entirely from the world around us we will have no opportunity to make an impact upon it. We cannot avoid seeing and hearing things that offend us, and there is no sin involved so long as we do not gladly receive those impressions or dwell on them. We need to ask the Lord's help in this and to help ourselves by taking every opportunity to fix our minds on things that are clean and wholesome. (Rom. 12:1-2; 2 Cor. 10: 3-5; Phil. 4:8)

I have heard it said that the sealing of the Spirit is an experience to be received after we are born again. Is this right?

As the Holy Spirit continues his work in us he sometimes gives us special experiences when we are overwhelmed with the presence of God and vividly aware of his holiness and love. The reason for such visitations may be to equip us for some work for him or to give us greater assurance of our salvation. Often these are painful and humbling experiences but they usually result in greater joy in the Lord than we had before.

Some Christians call an experience of this kind a sealing or a baptism of the Holy Spirit. In these studies we have taken the view that the baptism of the Spirit is when we are born again, and we are at the same time sealed as God's possession by the continuing residence of the Spirit. After this we may have special times of blessing of all kinds and we should expect and pray for such exalted experiences which the Lord may give us according to his wisdom. It does not matter what name we use so long as we do not close our minds to these wonderful possibilities. (1 Cor. 2:9-10)

QUESTIONS ASKED ABOUT STUDY 15

 I hear Christian people talk about revival. What does this mean?

 There are times in personal spiritual experience and in the history of churches when the Lord makes his presence felt in a specially powerful way. The effect on Christians is an intensification of grief for sin and also of delight in the certainty of God's love and mercy. This in turn makes an impact on the surrounding community as a fear of God comes on the people and many more than usual are converted.

 I do not think I could keep up the Christian life.

 You are quite right! No-one can sustain a life that is pleasing to God in their own strength. The Christian life is only possible because it is lived by the power of the Holy Spirit. It is not that the Lord does everything for us, but that he enables us to persevere. 'I can do everything through him who gives me strength' (Phil. 4:13, see also Jude 24-25; John 10:27-30).

 I tried it once and it didn't work.

 Most probably what you thought would happen was not at all what the Lord has promised. Also it is very likely that what you "tried" was not Christianity but Christianity in your own strength. True Christianity begins with being accepted by God through Jesus Christ. It is quite impossible for anyone to seek God's forgiveness on the basis of what Jesus Christ has done and to be rejected (John 6:37). When you begin there, you have God's promise he will enable you to go on to the end (Isa. 43:1-2). You will often fail miserably and even begin to despair; 'If we claim to be without sin, we deceive ourselves and the truth is not in us. If we confess our sins, he is faithful and just and will forgive us our sins and purify us from all unrighteousness' (1 John 1:8-9).

CHALLENGES from STUDY 15

 Is there something God is telling you to do that you are not willing to do? What is it?

 Do you think you are trusting more than trying or trying more than trusting?

 Write down further questions on this subject you will ask your group leader or Christian friend.

ACTION

 Learn and/or write down 1 John 3:1-3.
Is there a text in the Bible that has special meaning to you?
What is the text and the meaning?

STUDY 16

THE HOLY SPIRIT – GIVES STRENGTH FOR THE FIGHT

Reading: *Ephesians 6:10-20*

vv 10-11   In our fight against evil we are not strong enough in ourselves,
            we need to draw on the Holy Spirit's power.

v 12   The enemy we see is the temptation that comes to us through people,
            "flesh and blood" in one way or another, but behind what we see is
            Satan and whole host of his forces striving to deceive and defeat us.

v 13   When we are under spiritual attack it is too late to build up our
            defences. We must prepare ourselves well in advance of the onslaught
            so that we are not taken by surprise or easily overthrown.

vv 14-17   Our defensive weapons are knowledge of the truth, complete trust in
            Jesus Christ for acceptance with God ("rightness"), assurance of peace
            with God, a lively faith and confidence in the security ("salvation") we
            have in Jesus Christ.

vv 17-20   Our offensive weapons are the Scriptures and prayer, by these alone
            can Satan be defeated.

" O Father, I didn't realise Satan is real, I want to be a strong Christian. "

When we are unable to help ourselves the Lord will fight for us - but normally he expects us to fight - in his strength	Deut. 3:22; Neh. 4:20; Judg. 7:19-21; 1 Tim. 6:11-12
WE MUST • fight against sin in ourselves	Rom. 8:12-14; Gal. 5:16-17; Eph. 4:22
• resist the devil and his temptations	Matt. 26:41; Jas. 4:7; 1 Pet 5:9
• be like soldiers in an army opposed to evil and error	2 Cor. 10: 3-5; 2 Tim. 2:1-5; 4:7-8

• separate ourselves from the ungodly life-style of the world	Titus 2:11-12; 1 John 2:15-17
• be willing not to please ourselves but to suffer for Christ's sake	Phil. 1:29; 1 Thess. 4:1
• take up our cross - denying ourselves	Luke 9:23-25

In all our painful experiences - our Father

• is using them to purify and strengthen us	Heb. 12:4-11; 1 Peter 1:6-7
• is our refuge, sustainer and comfort	Ps. 46; John 16:33; Rom. 8:35-39

" Lord, thank you there is a purpose in all our struggles. "

QUESTIONS ASKED ABOUT STUDY 16

Why do some Christians seem to suffer more than others?

This is a fact of life and we must leave the reasons to the wisdom of our heavenly Father. (Read 2 Tim. 3:12) Such suffering is not necessarily chastisement for personal sin as the Book of Job makes clear. God knows all about each of us and how best to deal with us as his children; he knows what he wants to do with us and how he will teach others through his dealings with us.

Is it sinful to be tempted?

It is not sinful to be confronted with a choice to do right or wrong. But at the point where we want to do what is wrong we are sinning. We may pull back from the sinful act, but we still need the Lord's forgiveness for desiring the wrong.

If I succumb to temptation will God be angry with me?

Before we became Christians, God was our judge and we were under his wrath leading in the end to final judgement. As Christians, God is our Father who will be grieved by our sins and who will correct and chastise us, but with a view to glory not final judgement. This is a most important distinction for us to be sure about for our peace of mind. We must hold on to Rom. 8:1.

This study is all about fighting and struggling. I thought the Christian life was supposed to be peaceful and restful.

As we saw in **Study 15** we are both to trust and to try. As we do so our trusting will give us peace of mind and heart while at the same time we fight and struggle. A soldier will fight best when his mind is at rest and this is true in the spiritual conflict also. For a helpful illustration notice that as the word "rest" is inside the word "wRESTle", so while we wrestle against sin we must rest in Christ for our salvation. If we do not rest in this way we will soon begin to think we are fighting for our salvation instead of fighting because we are saved.

QUESTIONS ASKED ABOUT STUDY 16

 My faith is very weak and I am afraid I shall be defeated.

 Good! We are in real danger when we think our faith is strong and we are capable of meeting any challenge. One of the biggest mistakes we make is to trust in our faith instead of in the Lord. We can be making this mistake without realising it and the Lord sometimes helps us by making us face a situation that we cannot cope with so we learn how to rely on him alone. Let your sense of weakness drive you closer to the Lord and you will discover what Paul meant in 2 Cor. 12:10 'When I am weak, then I am strong.'

 There are some sins that seem impossible to deal with. I try hard and I am sure God can help me, but I still get defeated and there is no end to my battle.

 Be sure you are not alone! Every one who takes the Christian life seriously knows what you mean. Sin is deceitful and persistent and even if you think you have gained a victory, the enemy often returns just when you least expect. (See Gal. 5:16-17)
Some sins drop off immediately or soon after we are converted; others we overcome in course of time with the Lord's strength. But the Lord seems to leave us with a problem that keeps us humble and drives us to despair. We must not give up praying over this or lose our strong desire to get the victory. We must continue every means we know to help to rid ourselves of the problem. A close Christian friend or an effective small prayer group to which we may belong can be very helpful. We should be humble and desperate enough to share our problem and ask the help and prayer of our friends. This will also have the effect of making the fellowship even closer. But be careful; don't weary others with a constant harping on your problem, and don't air publicly things that should be kept to the closest relationships. Husbands and wives are in a good position to help each other in these things, but often they do not!

 I know I should hate sin, but if I am honest I have to admit there are some sins I do not hate.

 This confirms the Scripture 'The heart is deceitful above all things and beyond cure'. (Jer. 17:9.) Charles Wesley was a very godly man and yet he prayed "take away the love of sinning". The Christian life is so often like walking a tightrope. We must understand that we will never be entirely rid of the old nature and its deceptions until we reach heaven, but at the same time we should not settle for anything less than aiming for perfection here and now. We must hold these two things together: if we lose the first we will despair, but if we lose the second we will soon become careless and grieve the Holy Spirit. If we had easy or total victory we would soon fall into sinful pride. The Lord gives us many triumphs to keep us hopeful but not so many that we become complacent.

CHALLENGES from STUDY 16

 What temptations are especially strong for you?

 How are you involved in the fight against evil and falsehood in the world?

 Write down further questions on this subject you will ask your group leader or Christian friend.

ACTION

 Learn and/or write down Ephesians 6:10-12.
Take one daily newspaper and identify the evil in the world we must fight.

STUDY 17
THE HOLY SPIRIT – LEADS US ON

Reading: *Ephesians 4:22-5:2*

Throughout these verses notice how we are to abandon our old way of life and equally to begin living in a new way.

vv 22-24   The process is like taking off dirty and worn out clothes and putting on a clean outfit. This is not a mere outward show because it arises from an entirely new way of thinking. The aim is God-likeness.

v 25   Dishonesty gives place to trustworthiness.

vv 26-27   The devil will take advantage of simmering bitterness, so we must put things right with others and with God before the day ends.

v 28   Stealing must be replaced by good deeds.

v 29   Empty talk must give way to constructive and helpful conversation.

vv 30-5:2   Bitterness and malice grieve the Holy Spirit whose ministry is to rid us of such things. They must be discarded as filth and rubbish. In their place we are to be godly having Jesus Christ as the perfect example.

" Dear Father, I don't know what the future will be for me, how can I be sure you will be with me? "

The positive aim of the Christian life is to be like Jesus Christ	Rom. 8:28-29; Phil. 2:5; 1 Pet 2:20-23

For this we need the help of our Lord himself through the Holy Spirit   John 15:5

"Do not put out the Spirit's fire" (1 Thess. 5:19)

"Do not grieve the Holy Spirit of God" (Eph. 4:30)

"Be filled with the Spirit" (Eph. 5:18)

Christ-likeness is the result of the Spirit's work in us	2 Cor. 3:17-18; Gal. 5:22-23

This is a life

OF DISCIPLESHIP

obedience to Christ	Luke 8:19-21; John 14:15,21-24; Rom. 6:15-18
following Christ	John 10:26-31
self denial	Mark 8:34-37
caring	Luke 10:25-37
service	Matt 6:24; Gal. 5:13-14

OF PLEASING GOD

in personal life	John 5:30; Col. 1:9-10
in church life	Phil. 2:1-5
in family life	Eph. 5:22; 6:4
in community life	Rom. 13:1-7

OF WITNESSING TO OTHERS
Acts 1:8; 1 Thess. 1:6-8

OF GUIDANCE
Prov. 3:5-6; Rom. 12:1-2

OF PERSEVERANCE

we are assured of our entry into Glory	Rom. 8:28-30; Phil. 1:6
but we are commanded to persevere	Heb. 10:23; 12:1-2

QUESTIONS ASKED ABOUT STUDY 17

Where does the baptism of the Holy Spirit come in the Christian life?

In **Study 13** we have taken the view that the baptism of the Spirit occurs when we are born again. But some Christians apply the term to a profound spiritual experience after conversion. We have dealt with this along with the sealing of the Spirit in **question 3 Study 15**.

How can I be filled with the Spirit?

It is important to remember that in Eph. 5:18 the requirement to be filled with the Spirit is continuous - it is the level at which we should be living all the time. This depends on our constant and diligent application to prayer, meditation, obedience to the Scriptures in every aspect of life. This will include earnest prayer that the Lord will fill us with his Spirit at all times and especially when we face the challenges of Christian service. The Lord will respond to these requests according to his will for us. But we should not expect a "slot-machine" answer - prayer followed by immediate filling. As in everything God does things in his own way and time.

Do I need to be able to speak in tongues?

It is quite certain that this is not necessary as either a condition or proof of your salvation. We are saved 'by grace ... through faith' (Eph. 2:8) and absolutely nothing must be added to that. The proof of our salvation is not an ability to exercise any spiritual gift but in perseverance in holy living. Christian teachers are divided as to what is meant by speaking in tongues and its usefulness. Be sure to receive careful biblical teaching before coming to your own conclusion.

How does the Lord guide us?

For the most part guidance consists of obedience to the commands of Scripture. Where there is no direct command we can usually apply biblical principles to our situation, for example, such texts as 2 Cor. 6:14-7:1 and 1 Thess. 4:1-8 will lead us to God honouring decisions on widely differing occasions. The more we are saturated with Scripture and lovingly submissive to the Lord, the more we shall have the "mind of Christ" (Rom. 12:1-2, 1 Cor. 2:15-16, Phil. 2:5) and will know instinctively what the Lord wants us to do.
When we are confronted with particularly difficult decisions it is often helpful to consult a trustworthy, mature Christian. (Prov. 15:22, 20:18)

I have heard it said that we become Christians in two stages receiving Jesus Christ as Saviour first and then yielding to him as Lord later on. Is this right?

No! Jesus Christ is never other than both Lord and Saviour. A large part of the process of sanctification is obedience to Jesus Christ as our Lord, and as we have seen (**Study 14**) that process begins immediately we are born again.
So far is the idea in this question wrong, it completely reverses the order the apostle Peter repeatedly used (Acts 2:36; 2 Peter 1:11; 2:20; 3:18)

QUESTIONS ASKED ABOUT STUDY 17

How can I witness for Jesus Christ?

First by what you are. Your changed life and its quality will speak for itself and may well give rise to questions requiring you to say what has happened to you. Second, by what you say, and this order is most important (what you are speaks so loudly I can't hear what you say). You can give the Christian point of view in any discussion. You can challenge people about their relationship with God telling them what Jesus Christ means to you. Third, by acts of kindness. Fourth, by church attendance and serving the Lord through the church in its evangelistic programme.

Will God use me if I have sin in my life?

If he did not, none of us could be used! But God is offended by unconfessed sin that we are not seeking to overcome. Also neglect of prayer and attention to Scripture are common reasons for lack of usefulness. In practice we should not be surprised if obvious sins and faults negate what we try to say. For example, pride, a bad reputation or shoddy workmanship create barriers between us and those we are speaking to.

Is it possible for a Christian to be lost eternally?

No - because the Lord has promised to keep his people: he gives them eternal life and assures them they will never perish (John 10:27-30): they are united to Jesus Christ and are as secure as he is (Col. 3:1-4) and they are under God's covenant in which he pledges never to remember their sins because of what Jesus Christ has done for them (Heb. 10:17 see also Rom. 8:1).

Isn't it a fact that some Christians do depart from the Christian life and even renounce their faith?

This appears to be so, but
- such people may not have been true Christians despite appearances. The Bible constantly warns of the danger of looking like Christians and yet deceiving ourselves and others (Matt.13:18-23; Acts 8:9-24; Heb. 6:4-6);
- such people may be spiritually ill. Physically we can be so ill as to look as though we are dead and yet later recover. Similarly a true Christian may become spiritually sick and become like someone who is not a Christian, and yet later recover to full spiritual vigour. An example of this is the apostle Peter who denied the Lord in the strongest possible way and yet he later became a courageous leader in the early church (Luke 22:54-62; Acts 2:14; 1 Peter 1:1).

All this teaches us that while we rely on the Lord's promises and assurances we must never presume on God's mercy by becoming spiritually careless (Heb. 12:14-17).

CHALLENGES from STUDY 17

 What aspect of Christ-likeness do you find most challenging?

 Are you willing to be obedient to Jesus Christ in every area of your life? Is there any aspect of life you are unwilling to submit to the Lord's control?

 How bold is your witness to others? What more could you do to make Jesus Christ known?

 Write down further questions on this subject you will ask your group leader or Christian friend.

ACTION

 Learn and/or write down Romans 12:1-2.
Find out in the church you attend who has been a Christian for the longest time and ask him or her what has been the greatest help.

STUDY 18
THE HOLY SPIRIT – UNITES US TO GOD'S PEOPLE

Reading: *Acts 2:36-42*

vv 36-37   This chapter tells of the descent of the Holy Spirit and the sermon preached by the apostle Peter. His conclusion was to declare Jesus Christ as God's promised Messiah and therefore the one to be trusted, loved and obeyed. As a result many people became painfully aware of their spiritual need.

vv 38-39   Peter told them to repent. This would include turning from their sins and trusting in Jesus Christ for pardon. This repentance and faith was to be expressed openly in baptism and the Holy Spirit would at the same time be the proof and seal of their salvation.

vv 40-41   Baptism was the way of entry into the church at Jerusalem. There was a recognisable number of "members" to which new converts were added.

v 42   Their life together consisted of four elements.

   i)   Receiving sound teaching and keeping to it.

   ii)   Sharing together their spiritual experience and thus strengthening one another ("fellowship").

   iii)   Remembering the Lord's death by observing the Lord's Supper ("breaking of bread").

   iv)   Prayer – including praise and thanksgiving, prayer for others and for the progress of the gospel.

" Father, there is a lot of confusion about the church, please show me what a church should be like."

In the Bible "church" means either the total number of believers universally or a local gathering of believers

The ***universal church*** – is the total number of people who have been, are or will be saved from sin and its consequences through faith in Jesus Christ   Rev. 7:9-10

"God placed all things under his (Jesus Christ's) feet and appointed him to be head over everything for the church, which is his body, the fulness of him who fills everything in every way." (Eph. 1:22-23)

This universal church is likened to a

• body - of which Christ is the Head	1 Cor. 12:13
• bride	Eph. 5:25-27
• household/family	Eph. 2:19; 1 Tim. 3:5
• priesthood - all have direct access to God through Jesus Christ	1 Peter 2:4-5
• temple	Eph. 2:20-22
• city	Eph. 2:19
• nation/kingdom	Col. 1:12-14; 1 Peter 2:9

 This universal church cannot be destroyed and will be complete and perfect when Jesus Christ returns   Rev. 21:1-4

The *local church* — is a reflection of the universal
                  church in a local area   1 Cor. 12:12-26

"Now you are the body of Christ, and each one of you is a part of it". (1 Cor. 12:27)

All believers should be members   Acts 2:40-41

All members should be believers   1 Cor. 1:2

A local church must submit to Jesus Christ as its Head Col. 1:18

 NOTE: A church is therefore independent of all other authority whether civil or religious.

A local church should provide for

• teaching	1 Tim. 4:11-13
• evangelism	Acts 13:1-4
• worship	Heb. 13:15; 1 Peter 2:5
• fellowship	Acts 2:42
• caring	Acts 2:44
• discipline	Matt 18:15-20; 1 Cor. 5:1-5
• baptism	Matt 28:19
• Lord's Supper	Acts 2:46

A local church is a means of Christian
growth into holiness.   Eph. 4:11-13

A local church has the promise of Jesus Christ's
presence when it gathers.   Matt 18:20

" Father, thank you for your churches all over the world."

QUESTIONS ASKED ABOUT STUDY 18

May I be a member of the universal church and not bother with a local one?

The New Testament assumes all believers are members of local churches. The clear example is Acts 2:36-42 and following that we see letters being addressed to churches. But the bigger question is, Why do you not want to be a member of a local church? Do you not want to be a blessing to other Christians, serve with other Christians, have the benefit of the sanctifying effect of church life, receive a regular biblical ministry or submit to the discipline of elders?

The Lord blesses churches that submit a central organisation, so why insist that local churches should be independent?

The Lord blesses whom he will. We are to obey him to the best of our knowledge and ability, not because we hope for greater "success" but because that is our responsibility. The words of Deut.29:29 provide the answer to all such questions.

Why are so few churches today like those in the New Testament?

All churches fall short of the New Testament ideal to some degree because the leaders and members are imperfect people. But we should remember that the churches in those days also had their problems as a reading of 1 Cor. would show. It is a greater problem when churches do not realise they need constant reformation in the light of Scripture.

What should I do if there is no church I am happy with near where I live?

This is a problem for which you may need the help of mature Christian friends. We certainly should join a church as near as possible to where we live. We need also to consider our own spiritual needs and those of our children. If we feel the Lord is calling us to exert an influence in an "unsound" church, we need to ask ourselves if we are spiritually strong enough to survive being deprived of regular profitable ministry and fellowship.

Why do you not believe in bishops?

A bishop with responsibility over a whole area of churches may appear to be more efficient and provide support for local pastors and churches. But there is no such provision in the New Testament, where each local church had a number of overseers (bishops AV). Most independent churches are in fact linked with some kind of inter-church organisation to co-ordinate their work and give mutual support.

Why are there so many divisions among Christians?

Christians are not perfect; they are on the way to perfection but meantime their old nature continues to do a lot of damage. Some divisions are caused by pride, jealousy and lack of love. This grieves the Holy Spirit and hinders the work of the gospel. Some "denominational" differences are caused by the same sinful attitudes while others are the result of adherence to traditions instead of a constant reference to Scripture and reformation by its teaching.

There is a clear and necessary division between those churches that submit to the Bible (evangelicals) and those who do not (liberals). Evangelicals are united on the basic teaching in our **Studies 1-12.** They have considerable agreement on the main lines of **Studies 13-23**, but differ in their understanding of some aspects of the work of the Holy Spirit, the administration of churches and of the events surrounding the personal return of Jesus Christ. The unity of evangelical Christians eclipses and overcomes their differences that arise from our inability to interpret the Scriptures perfectly.

Surely the churches are full of hypocrites?

There are certainly hypocrites in the churches as in any other part of life and we know what Jesus Christ thinks about them (Matt 7:21-23, 23:13-33). But this assertion generally arises from a misunderstanding. People who go to church are thought by that act to be making themselves out to be better than others when everybody knows they are not. But people should go to church because they know they are sinful and need the Lord's help. The church is not a house of saints but a school for sinners. This is not to excuse hypocrisy, but to deny that the churches are "full of frauds." There are less hypocrites in the churches than there are among those who make statements like this one.

CHALLENGES from STUDY 18

 Are you a member of a local church? If not why not?

 What is the most important part of church life you have or look forward to?

 What difficulties, if any, do you have in joining a local church?

 Write down further questions on this subject you will ask your group leader or Christian friend.

ACTION

 Learn and/or write down Ephesians 4:11-13.
Find the person in the church you attend who has been longest in membership and ask him or her to give you a brief outline of its history in their lifetime.

STUDY 19
THE HOLY SPIRIT – DIRECTS THE CHURCHES (1)

Reading: *Romans 12:1 - 16*

vv 1-2   In the light of all that God has done for us through our Lord Jesus
            Christ we must give ourselves to him and try to please him in every
            aspect of life.

vv 3-5   One of these aspects is church life. Our attitudes and activities
            within our church fellowship must be in accordance with Scripture.
            Here the requirement is humbly regarding ourselves as no more
            important than any other member, and reckoning it our privilege
            to serve one another.

vv 6-8   Whatever our gifts or the work we do in the church we must do it
            enthusiastically and to the best of our ability.

vv 9-13   If one thing is as important as humility it is love expressed cheerfully
            in both words and deeds.

vv 14-16   Humility and love will involve sympathy in which we try to understand
            other people's feelings and share those feelings with them. This applies
            to our relationship with all members of the church no matter what
            their intellect or social standing may be.

" Dear Lord, if I join a church I want to be a help not a hindrance."

**A local church is a living body of which Jesus Christ
is the Head**   Rom. 12:5

> *"Speaking the truth in love, we will in all things grow up into
> him who is the Head, that is, Christ. From him the whole body,
> joined and held together by every supporting ligament, grows
> and builds itself up in love, as each part does its work." (Eph. 4:15-16)*

NOTE: This means it is not a democratic organisation like a social club or a
            local council committee

A local church is led by elders assisted by deacons   Acts 14:23;
                                                             Phil. 1:1

NOTE: In the New Testament elders are also pastors   1 Tim. 3:1-13;
            (shepherds) and overseers (bishops AV)   1 Peter 5:1-3

STUDY 19 Continued

A local church receives direction from Jesus Christ as Head

    by the Holy Spirit's leading through the Scriptures   Acts 15:13-29;

    by the whole church led by the elders   20:17, 28-32

Elders and deacons are expected to

- lead the church   1 Thess. 5:12-13
- love the church   Phil. 2:25-26
- teach the church   1 Tim. 3:2
- serve the church   Matt. 20:25-28
- care for the church   1 Tim. 3:5
- train the church for service   Eph. 4:11-25

Members of the church are expected to

- share the gospel with others   Acts 8:4
- love each other   John 13:34-35; Phil. 2:1-4
- submit to each other   Eph. 5:21
- serve each other   Gal. 5:13; 1 Peter 4:10
- attend the meetings (for worship, prayer and fellowship)   Heb. 10:24-25
- support the work financially   1 Cor. 16:1-2
- pray for each other   Eph. 6:18-20
- respect the leaders   Heb. 13:17
- help in the work   Matt. 25:14-30

" Dear Father, it is more difficult than I realised to be a good church member. Please make me willing"

QUESTIONS ASKED ABOUT STUDY 19

How do churches make decisions?

Each church has its own procedure. Traditionally, independent churches have adopted a democratic procedure in which the Lord's will is believed to be made known by a majority vote, but a majority is not always right. More recently there has been more emphasis on the leadership of the elders.

Ideally the elders lead in such a way as to involve the whole church by a process of consultation and discussion. It is the leaders who will answer to the Lord (Heb. 13:17) but this does not give them the right to dictate to the church. The humblest member may have a valuable contribution to make on the issue under consideration. In seeking the mind of the Lord the leaders must, on the one hand, avoid expecting the church to "rubber stamp" their recommendations without question, and on the other hand failing to exercise leadership based on biblical principles. Even when a majority accepts certain ideas, it may not be wise immediately to act on it.

What can members do if they disagree with decisions?

Everything depends on whether the matter involves a clear biblical principle. If it does not, then it should be possible to accept the decision with Christian grace. If there is no doubt that a biblical principle is involved then there should be prayerful discussion with the elders. This process should be given plenty of time to bear fruit. Hasty threats to resign must be avoided and no effort spared to reconcile differences. But if this fails, guidance should be sought as to whether to withdraw from the church. Whatever happens we are clearly instructed to 'do everything without complaining or arguing'. (Phil. 2:14)

What is the difference between an elder and a deacon?

In Acts 6:1-6 men were appointed to relieve the apostles of things that took them away from "prayer and the ministry of the Word" and deacons are their successors. Detailed qualifications of elders are found in 1 Tim. 3: 1-7 and Titus 1:6-9, and of deacons in 1 Tim. 3: 8-13. A distinctive quality of elders is that they are "able to teach" (1 Tim. 3:2).

Sometimes it is said that elders are responsible for spiritual matters and deacons for the material business. This is a useful guide so long as we remember that all church business must be done in a spiritual manner, and that deacons are by no means excluded from spiritual ministry (e.g. visiting the elderly). Elders and deacons provide a focal point for the ministry of the whole church and at the same time they should seek to harness all the gifts and talents of the members.

QUESTIONS ASKED ABOUT STUDY 19

 How can a member leave a church?

 If there is really no alternative then everything must be done in love and humility and in a way that causes least damage to the honour of Christ, the peace of the church and to the spiritual health of those concerned.

It is very unsatisfactory simply to stop attending and without warning or adequate reason to move to another church. The matter should be discussed at length with the elders with a view to reconsideration or a commendation to another fellowship. This is better than going through a period without church membership.

 How can I know what God wants me to do in the church?

 Examine yourself to discover your strengths and weaknesses and then offer the best you can do for service in the church. You may see a need in the church you know you can meet; do not wait to be asked, offer to help, but be willing to accept the decision of the elders if for some reason they decline your offer. The church may invite you to serve in some way and if at all possible you should agree. If you feel unsuited to that particular task remember, others can often assess us better than we can ourselves, and the Lord is able to help you to do better than you think possible.

 Do I really have to love every member of the church?

 Yes! It is the Lord's command, you have no option (John 15:12). If this is difficult do not forget other people may not find it easy to love you. We may not be attracted naturally to others in the church, and they may not be drawn to us. But we are required to unite with all members in the work of the gospel, to pray for all, to care for all and to be concerned for the spiritual health of all the members. We are to forgive others their faults and failings. These requirements are good for all and essential for our sanctification Be sure to make it easy for others to love you.

I have been told I should give a tenth of my income to the church. Is this right?

This is called "tithing" and it means setting aside a tenth of our total income for the Lord's work. The larger part of this may be given to one's church but a proportion is reserved for other good causes such as missionary work, Christian healing and caring ministries etc. The tenth is to be regarded as a minimum not a maximum of our total giving. The practice is based on Old Testament examples (Gen. 14:20, 28:22, Num. 18:21-24, Deut. 12:4-7). Some Christians believe we are still to observe these laws and that this is an obligation. Others believe these laws as such are no longer binding on us, but that nevertheless because of all Christ's love means to us we should not give less than the Old Testament law required. It is right to say that all we have belongs to the Lord, but that can be such a vague idea that in practice it leads to poor giving. For some people a tithe may still leave them with far more than they need. But in other situations tithing is difficult, unwise or even impossible (e.g. little or no income; total dependence on the state; a married Christian whose partner is not sympathetic). Some basic teaching on this subject is found in 2 Cor. 8 where we find the Macedonian churches giving 'as much as they were able, and even beyond their ability' (v 3).

CHALLENGES from STUDY 19

 If you are not a member of a church and hesitating to become one, why is this?

 Are you willing to submit yourself to a church and its leaders? If not, why not?

 What gift or talent do you have that would be useful in church life?

 Write down further questions on this subject you will ask your group leader or Christian friend.

ACTION

 Learn and/or write down Romans 12:9-11. Ask for a copy of the "rules" of the church you attend and find out if they are adhered to.

STUDY 20
THE HOLY SPIRIT – DIRECTS THE CHURCHES (2)

Church life must be shaped by the Holy Spirit through the Scriptures   2 Tim. 3:16-17

The Scriptures give us two – and only two – symbols to observe, Believers' Baptism and the Lord's Supper

Believers' Baptism

Reading: *Acts 8:26-39*

vv 26-29   There were many non-Jewish (Gentiles) attracted to the Jewish religion, some of whom were pilgrims to Jerusalem. (Acts 2:7-11)

vv 30-31   These people studied the Old Testament and learned to believe in the one true God and his promises through the prophets.

vv 32-33   It is not surprising the eunuch was puzzled because the Jews themselves found it hard to believe their Messiah would be a suffering servant. This was one of the reasons they had Jesus Christ crucified.

vv 34-35   Philip not only told the eunuch that Isaiah's prophecy was about Jesus Christ, but that his death in the place of sinful people was the good news.

vv 36-37   Philip must also have included the requirement of baptism for believers as the symbol of abandoning all other hope except trust in Jesus Christ alone.

vv 38-39   The description of baptism given here is consistent with immersion for which they both went down into the water.

" O Lord, baptism seems to be turning my back on the past, please help me to do that."

"Go and make disciples of all nations, baptising them in the name of the Father and of the Son and of the Holy Spirit." (Matt. 28:19)

Believers' Baptism is

• for believers only   Acts 2:41; 16:14-15

           Therefore   –   it is not a means of salvation
                           –   not for babies

• immersion - (as the Greek word consistently means)   Col. 2:12
• a command to the church   Matt. 28:19-20;
                                                                                     Acts 10:47-48

• symbolic of
           cleansing   Heb. 10:22
           baptism in the Spirit   1 Cor. 12:13
           renunciation of the past   Rom. 6:2-5
• the normal entry into church life   Acts 2:41

STUDY 20 Continued

The Lord's Supper

Reading: *Luke 22:14-20*

vv 14-18   Before our Lord was crucified he wanted to observe the Passover in which they remembered the miraculous deliverance of the Israelites from Egyptian slavery (Exod. 12:1-13). This deliverance depended on a lamb's blood being painted around their doorways. Jesus Christ is called "the lamb of God" (John 1:29) because through his blood we are saved from the slavery of sin.

v 19   The first of the two parts in the Lord's Supper is breaking bread and eating a small portion of it together. This symbolises the breaking of our Lord's body at his crucifixion.

NOTE: Since Jesus was himself handling the bread *"this is my body"* cannot mean it has been literally changed into himself. He meant, *"this represents my body"*.

v 20   The second part is the pouring out of wine and taking a sip of it together. This symbolises the blood of Jesus by which we are saved. The new covenant is God's promise to forgive all who trust in his Son (Heb. 10:11-18). God confirmed his covenant with the sprinkling of blood (Exod. 24:8)

The Lord's Supper is

     • commanded for all believers   1 Cor. 11:23

     • a means of remembering what Jesus Christ
       has done for us   1 Cor. 11:24-25

     • a means of seeking and expressing the unity
       of the church   1 Cor. 10:14-17;
                                                1 Cor. 11:17-29

Believers' Baptism has to do with the beginning of the Christian life

The Lord's Supper has to do with the continuing life of a believer

This will normally determine the order in which they are observed

> " O Lord, prepare me for the big step; I want to be right with you."

QUESTIONS ASKED ABOUT STUDY 20

 Can we be Christians without being baptised?

 Yes, but disobedient Christians!

 Isn't baptism a personal decision?

 It is the responsibility of the church to provide for baptism, preach it, practise it and decide who is qualified for it. Converted people should offer themselves for baptism responding to the command 'Repent and be baptised every one of you' (Acts 2:38). Baptism should never be thought of as an option to be decided upon but rather as a command to be obeyed. (Acts 10:47-48)

 What is the basis of infant sprinkling?

 There are many explanations given by those who practise infant sprinkling, but the most common is based on the idea that baptism is the New Testament replacement of circumcision. The two are found together in Col. 2:11-12. The reasoning is that since circumcision was for male infants then baptism must also be for infants – male and female, and like circumcision, is a sign of the covenant. Arguments for sprinkling range from a supposed lack of water in Jerusalem on the day of Pentecost, the difference in temperature between Palestine and other countries, to questions about the meaning of the word translated "baptism" in the New Testament. Those holding to Believers' Baptism see the New Testament fulfilment of circumcision in regeneration (Phil. 3:3, Rom. 2:28-29); they understand that baptism is for those who are already regenerate (Acts 9:17-19).

QUESTIONS ASKED ABOUT STUDY 20

I am willing to be baptised but not to join the church.

To take this position is to fly in the face of the pattern laid down for us immediately after Pentecost in Acts 2:36-42. But why make this proviso?

Since baptism is commanded and church membership is certainly the pattern of the New Testament, it is hardly right to submit to one without the other. We need the fellowship of a church and other members need us; to deprive them and ourselves of this benefit is unsatisfactory to say the least.

Must I be baptised before I can take the Lord's Supper?

There is no doubt that the order in Scripture is Believer's Baptism followed by the Lord's Supper (see the key passage — Acts 2: 36-42) and most people agree that this was the order in the early church.

How often should the Lord's Supper be observed?

There is no clear answer to this in Scripture. Some fellowships observe the Supper weekly, deducing this from Acts 20:7. Others arrange for this once or twice a month and even less frequently. The important thing is that the church provides for the Supper regularly, that all members share in it so far as is possible, and that the Lord's purposes in giving us this observance are fulfilled.

CHALLENGES from STUDY 20

 What have you learned about baptism you did not know before?

 Is baptism a problem to you? If so why?

 What effect do you think the Lord's Supper should have on the life of the church?

 Write down further questions on this subject you will ask your group leader or Christian friend.

ACTION

 Learn and/or write down Matthew 28:18-20.
As soon as possible attend a baptismal service and a Lord's Supper as an observer, and write down your impressions.

STUDY 21
JESUS CHRIST'S RETURN – PROMISES AND SIGNS

Reading: *Acts 1:1-11*

vv 1-3   During 40 days after his resurrection Jesus completed his instruction to his disciples.

vv 4-5   This teaching included the promise of the Holy Spirit.

vv 6-9   It also included a pointed reminder of their task after he had left them and returned to heaven.

vv 10-11   Jesus' ascension will by no means be the end of the story. He will come back to earth again in person.

> " Lord, I would like to know more about what is going to happen to the world."

The personal return of Jesus Christ will complete his work of undoing the effects of the 'Fall' - by releasing us from the world and the world from its frustration and corruption *(Look back to the note at the end of* **Study 7.***)*

By his death and resurrection he has dealt with the problem of our guilt and separation from God   } **Studies 8-12**

By his Spirit's power in our lives he deals with the corruption of sin in us that blights our conduct   } **Studies 13-20**

By his return he will rid the world entirely of sin and its effects on the whole of creation   } **Studies 21-22**

THE PROMISE   is that Jesus Christ will appear for a second time

- on earth   Titus 2:13; Heb. 9:27-28
- in person   John 14:1-3; Acts 1:11
- seen by all   Matt. 24:27; Rev. 1:7
- unexpected   Matt. 24:42-44; 1 Thess. 5:1-5
- a glorious sight   Matt. 24:30-31; 1 Thess. 4:16; 2 Thess. 2:8
- finally to defeat all his enemies   1 Cor. 15:20-25; 2 Thess. 2:5-12

NOTE: *"Like a thief in the night"(Matt. 24:42-44; 1 Thess. 5:1-11)* does not mean the Lord will come secretly but that his coming will be sudden and unexpected by unbelievers

The Signs of our Lord's return do not enable us to predict the future but to understand what is happening in the world

Some of the signs are

• increased lawlessness	Luke 17:26-30; 2 Tim. 3:1-5
• international friction	Matt. 24:6-8
• departure from the truth	Matt. 24:4-5; Acts 20:30
• fierce persecution	Matt. 24:9
• spiritism	1 Tim. 4:1
• worldwide gospel preaching	Matt. 24:14

NOTE: *"last days" (Acts 2:17; 2 Tim. 3:1; 2 Pet 3:3 1 John 2:18)*
is the whole period between Jesus' first and second comings.
Most probably the signs will intensify during this period

" Dear Lord, thank you for not leaving us in the dark about your plan for the world."

QUESTIONS ASKED ABOUT STUDY 21

Some people say that the coming again of Jesus is the gift of the Spirit and not a personal return. Is this right?

Many attempts are made to avoid the idea that Jesus will return in person. In addition to the one mentioned in the question it is suggested that the return of Jesus is when we have deep spiritual experiences, or that it is Jesus coming to meet us when we die. None of these explanations are sufficient to satisfy the clear meaning of Matt. 24:30-31; Acts 1:11; Heb. 9:27-28 and many more texts.

There is a theory that the history of the world is a sequence of circles — history repeating itself. Is this right?

Left to ourselves we can interpret human history in all kinds of ways. The main purpose of Ecclesiastes in the Old Testament is to show how one man tried all kinds of ideas to make sense of life without God. The Bible leaves us in no doubt that history is a straight line heading towards God's prescribed end. Look again at Heb. 9:27-28.

Is the return of the Jews to Palestine in recent years a sign that the coming of Jesus is near?

This is a view held by many Christians and they may be right. We all need to watch every possible sign as the Lord's plan unfolds. Reasons for not accepting this view are:

a)   All the Old Testament predictions about the people of Israel are said in the New Testament to be fulfilled spiritually in the church. (1 Peter 2:9-10)

b)   Jesus himself announced the end of the special position of the Jews in the plan of God. (Matt. 21:43; 23:37-38)

c)   Predictions in Scripture about the land of Palestine (Israel) are interpreted in terms of the spiritual inheritance of believers and the ultimate new heaven and new earth. (Heb. 11:8-10; 2 Peter 3:13)

Some Bible students also believe that before the Lord returns there will be a great worldwide spiritual revival arising out of a massive turning of the Jews to Christ. Again, this may be true but our understanding has to be shaped by a careful and detailed study of such Scriptures as Rom. chapters 9-11.

QUESTIONS ASKED ABOUT STUDY 21

 How would it be possible for everyone all over the world to see one person at one and the same time?

 Until recently Christians had to take such predictions on trust. But science has now discovered a way by satellite for us all to see the same event as it happens. This is not to say Jesus will appear on our television screens, but there is no longer any reason to doubt that what man can do God can do much more dramatically and gloriously.

 Will there be a revival of Christianity before the Lord returns?

 Bible students are divided on this question. Some see only increased persecution and departure from the faith (Matt. 24:4-13) while others anticipate a great time of revival (Matt. 13:31-32; Acts 3:19-21).

Experience teaches us that churches grow in numbers and spiritual vitality in times of opposition and suffering. It may be that both the pessimists and the optimists are right!

CHALLENGES from STUDY 21

 Read the parable in Matthew 25:1-13 and say how you think you should be ready for the Lord's return.

 Read the parable in Matt. 25:14-30 and say what you think you should be doing before the Lord returns.

 Write down further questions on this subject you will ask your group leader or Christian friend.

ACTION

 Learn and/or write down John 14:1-3.
Find out as many countries as you can where Christians today are being tortured because of their faith.

STUDY 22
JESUS CHRIST'S RETURN —THE END

Reading: *2 Peter 3:1-14*

vv 1-2   The whole Scripture (prophets and apostles) points on to an end time. This should lead us to think rightly about our present life.

vv 3-4   There have always been people who have jeered at the teaching given here because the end seems to be a long time coming.

vv 5-7   The story of the flood should be enough to convince us that God is certain to do what he has promised (or threatened) in his own way and time.

vv 8-9   In one sense we should be glad the Lord has not yet come because his delay is giving time for more people to be saved.

vv 10-14   The end will be the purging of the world by fire and the establishing of a new heaven and earth in which all the consequences of sin will be completely absent.

> " Lord, I want to believe that Jesus is coming back – help me to understand."

When Christ returns he will raise the dead

There is life after death	John 11:23-26; Heb. 2:14-15
At death the spirits of believers go immediately to the Lord	Luke 23:43; 2 Cor. 5:6-10
At death unbelievers are held for the day of judgement	2 Peter 2:9
Christ will raise all dead bodies and unite them with their spirits	John 5:28-30
The resurrection bodies of believers will be like Christ's resurrection body	1 Cor. 15:35-44; Phil. 3:17-21
Those who are alive when Christ comes will be changed and united with those who died	1 Thess. 4:13-17

Christ's return will bring the day of reckoning

Everyone will face God for judgement	Matt. 25:31-46; 2 Cor. 5:10
Believers will not be condemned	Rom. 8:1
Their works will be assessed and rewarded	1 Cor. 3:10-15
They will worship and serve the Lord for ever	Rev. 7:9-17
Unbelievers will be condemned - they will be punished for their sins	Rev. 20:11-15; Matt. 25:46

 Christ's return will bring the new heaven and earth

Sin and all its effects will be banished for ever	Rom. 8:18-21
Satan and all his helpers will be destroyed	Matt. 25:41; Rev. 20:10
Purity, peace, love and joy will prevail unabated	2 Peter 3:11-13; Rev. 22:1-5
God will reign unchallenged for ever	1 Cor. 15:21-28; Rev. 19:1-6

 "Lord, I can see that I need to prepare for Jesus Christ's return — make me serious about this."

QUESTIONS ASKED ABOUT STUDY 22

 Where do unbelievers go when they die?

 Our Lord's teaching in Luke 16:19-31 suggests that when unbelievers die they immediately begin to experience punishment for their sins and this seems to be confirmed by Heb. 9:27 and 2 Peter 2:4-9. We should take these Scriptures seriously and not speculate beyond them.

 The idea of hell and eternal punishment is hard to reconcile with a God of love.

 When Abraham was faced with a similar dilemma he found a resting place for his mind in this: 'Will not the Judge of all the earth do right?' (Gen. 18:25). The Bible clearly teaches both the love of God and eternal retribution for the unrepentant. (Matt. 25:46; 2 Thess. 1:5-10) There would be no hope for the suffering multitudes, nor meaning in this world of violence and oppression if there were to be no final reckoning and righting of wrongs. A world without judgement is not the world of a God of love. Some Christians accept the idea of judgement and punishment but not of eternal punishment. Attractive though this may seem to be, it is difficult to square it with the plain teaching of Scripture and especially of Jesus himself.

 How can we accept the idea that the world will be destroyed by fire?

 This is clearly predicted in 2 Peter 3:7,12, but until the end of the second world war people scoffed at the idea. However the coming of the nuclear age has shown us that such a thing is indeed terribly possible. This is not to say that the world will end by some human person pressing a button, perhaps by mistake, but we now see that a universal conflagration could easily take place, and this should be a warning to the present generation.

 What will resurrection bodies be like?

 Paul tells us they will be like our Lord's resurrection body (Phil. 3:21). We need to read the stories of what happened after Jesus rose from the dead at the end of each of the Gospels. There we see that he was not a ghost, his body was real, but he was able to appear and disappear from human view at will. At the same time he was recognisable, he could be touched, and he could eat food. This is not easy to imagine and even the disciples themselves had problems. In 1 Cor. 15:42-44 Paul likens resurrection bodies to something very beautiful which has grown from a seed that died.

QUESTIONS ASKED ABOUT STUDY 22

 It is difficult to believe in the resurrection of bodies that have been decomposed for centuries.

 'Is anything too hard for the Lord?' (Gen. 18:14)

 In the study there is no mention of a millennium that many people seem to believe in.

 The word "millennium" means a thousand years. It is true that some Bible students believe that when Jesus Christ comes again he will literally reign for a thousand years on the earth. This teaching is based on Rev. 20:1-4 and it may be the right way to understand this passage. But we should remember that the book of Revelation is full of symbols and therefore it is more likely that the thousand years is symbolic of a set period of time when Christ will reign – the time set by God and known only to him.

Some see this as a time of universal spiritual revival – Christ seen to be king in the church before he returns in person. Others believe this is another way of describing the present age between our Lord's first and second comings, during which he is ruling over his church and bringing her to her ultimate consummation, which is the view taken in this study.

 Will there be animals in heaven?

 The answer depends on the meaning of Isa. 11:6-9 and 65:25. If we take them literally the answer to the question is yes. But such passages are most probably pictures of a condition of peace and harmony; if that is right the answer is – we do not know. But, as a mother wisely told her child who had asked the same question – if we need them, they will be there!

 What about people who have never heard the gospel?

 The Bible does not give us a clear answer to this question. But there is no doubt that no-one in the whole world deserves to be saved, that the only way of salvation is through Jesus Christ and that the absence of faith in him leaves people under God's condemnation. There is no question here about God's justice since all without exception deserve his punishment, nor about God's right, in mercy and grace, to save some and not others.
We can be certain that none will be judged unfairly as Paul says 'All who sin apart from the law will also perish apart from the law, and all who sin under the law will be judged by the law' (Rom. 2:12). We can also be certain that our attitude to this problem should not be to doubt the justice and mercy of God, but to renew our support for, and engagement in every kind of missionary endeavour all over the world.

QUESTIONS ASKED ABOUT STUDY 22

Do "death experiences" of people who survive to tell us about them help us to believe in life after death and to understand what happens beyond the grave?

Not really. Those who were brought back to life by Jesus did not speak of their experience or add to our knowledge in any way. Jesus Christ is the only true guide in these matters.

In heaven will we recognise people we have known in this life?

The Bible does not answer this question directly, but there may be a clue in the story of our Lord's transfiguration (Luke 9:28-33) in which the disciples appear to have recognised Moses and Elijah who they had never seen before. This seems to suggest the answer is yes. Be sure if we need this kind of recognition it will not be denied us; nothing will mar our complete joy and contentment in heaven.

Surely there will be another chance for people to repent after death and before the judgement?

The Bible is clear that what we are when we die is what we will be at the judgement. (See Luke 16:19-31; Heb. 9:27). Nowhere in the Bible is there even a hint of a possible second chance, or of a place (some call purgatory) of cleansing and improvement between death and judgement. If we are trusting Christ now we are already accepted by God and will not be condemned (Rom. 8:1) – death will make no difference.

Is cremation wrong?

Arguments in favour of cremation are based on considerations of hygiene and space. Also many people prefer it because of its advantages in unsuitable weather and they prefer the procedure at the committal. The main reason why some Christians believe cremation to be wrong is the biblical prohibition of the burning of bodies (e.g. Deut. 12:29-31), but it would seem the reason for this was the need for the people of Israel not to copy idolatrous practices of other nations. Also cremation seems to them an unseemly desecration of the body. They point to the example of the burying of Jesus Christ and the comfort they derive from feeling that their loved one has been "laid to rest". It is certain that cremation makes no difference whatever to the resurrection because all the dead will be raised no matter what happened to their bodies.

CHALLENGES from STUDY 22

 Will you be among the inhabitants of the new heaven and earth? If so what grounds do you have for that expectation? If not, what are you going to do about it?

 What are you doing to rescue other people from God's judgement?

 Write down further questions on this subject you will ask your group leader or Christian friend.

ACTION

 Learn and/or write down 2 Peter 3:11-13. Find two people, one strongly in favour of cremation and the other very much against it and try to evaluate their arguments for yourself.

STUDY 23
WHAT NOW?

The Lord has been good in giving you the opportunity to discover what he wants you to know

This puts a great responsibility on you to do something about what you have learned

The story of Zaccheus has some pointers in the right direction

Reading:　　　　　*Luke 19:1-10*

v 1　　　*"Jesus entered Jericho and was passing through"* and there is no evidence that he went that way again.

　　　During these sessions the Lord has been very close to you. You must not assume that he will come so close to you again so now is the time for you to make your response to him. (2 Cor. 5:20-6:2)

vv 2-4　　　Zaccheus' curiosity about Jesus and his sense of need were enough for him to overcome all the obstacles to get a clear view of Jesus.

　　　Your spiritual need is so great that you should allow no obstacles to stand in the way of you seeking the Lord. It is not enough to know about him, you need a personal encounter with him.

v 5　　　This story gives us the distinct impression that Jesus went that way especially to meet Zaccheus.

　　　It should be a great encouragement to you to know that if you are keen to meet the Lord he is already on his way to you and is very willing to be found. He has promised that if you seek him you will find him. (Matt. 7:7-8)

v 6　　　The Lord called Zaccheus to come down from the tree where he was hiding and to meet him face to face and to do so immediately.

　　　You too must break loose from everything that keeps you apart from Jesus. Meet him in prayer as you confess your sins to him and tell him that you trust him alone as your Lord and Saviour. There is no time to lose; there are great dangers in delay – you may not have such an opportunity again. (Isa. 55:6-7)

STUDY 23 Continued

v 7   Jesus ignored the sneers of other people and so did Zaccheus as
he began to enjoy a new relationship with the Lord.

        You may be surrounded by people who reject the Lord and
sneer about all these things. But the Lord loves you and he
is willing to be identified with you and be your friend for life.
None of us deserves this.

v 8   This encounter with Jesus had the effect of intensifying Zaccheus'
sense of guilt about his sins and was the beginning of a process
of reformation.

        It will be similar to this for you. The first thing others may
know about your conversion will be your abandoning of
bad habits and sinful practices. You will put right bad
relationships and things you doted on before will begin to
take a lesser place in your life.

This is practical repentance and there are other examples in the Bible

Acts 16:33-34	the Philippian jailer washed his prisoners' wounds
Acts 19:17-20	Ephesian people destroyed their books on magic and the occult
Phil. 3:4-7	Paul stopped boasting in his advantages of birth and nationality

vv 9-10   Jesus said Zaccheus was "saved" because he was a "son of Abraham".
This meant he was not only physically descended from Abraham,
but had faith as did Abraham. Zaccheus' salvation did not rest
on the changes in his life but on his faith in the Lord.

If you have come to faith in the Lord Jesus Christ as your Lord and
your Saviour from sin and its consequences, then Jesus says to you
"salvation has come" to you. Look again at Eph. 2:8-9.

*"It is by grace you have been saved, through faith — and this not
from yourselves, it is the gift of God — not by works, so that
no-one can boast."*

The changes for the better in your life are evidence of the reality
of your faith.

Jesus will give you this assurance as you believe what God says about
those who trust his Son (John 3:36) and the Holy Spirit will give
you peace of mind that you are at peace with God through our Lord
Jesus Christ. (Rom. 5:1)

We are not told that Zaccheus was baptised but we do know that after Jesus went back to heaven and the Holy Spirit was given, the regular practice of the churches was to baptise those who came to faith in Jesus Christ: for example:

An Ethiopian official	Acts 8:36-39
Lydia of Philippi	Acts 16:13-15
The Jailer	Acts 16:31-34

This must surely be your next step, finishing with the old life and publicly confessing what the Lord has done for you.

" Lord, please make me sincere in my response to all you have done for me."

QUESTIONS ASKED ABOUT STUDY 23

My parents are opposed to my being baptised. What should I do?

Obey your parents unless or until you are free from parental control. The Scriptures tell us to "honour" our parents (Eph. 6:1-3) so even when you are free to be baptised, maintain a humble and tender attitude to them.

My fiancé is threatening to leave me if I am baptised. Must I go through with it?

Your first loyalty must be to the Lord. This may seem hard but it is better than a life-long marriage that is spiritually sterile. A single life is much happier than a divided marriage relationship, and the Lord has great blessings for those who deny themselves for his sake. (Luke 18:28-30)

I am afraid of the consequences of openly confessing Jesus Christ; why can't I be a secret disciple?

You need to think very carefully about what Jesus said "Whoever acknowledges me before men, I will also acknowledge him before my Father in heaven. But whoever disowns me before men, I will disown him before my Father in heaven". (Matt. 10:32-33)

How can I be sure I am a Christian?

Assurance that we are Christians can come to us in three ways:
- a) By believing what God says in the Bible about people who trust in Jesus Christ. (John 10:27-30; Rom. 8:1)

- b) By knowing that we have inward spiritual experience such as love to Jesus Christ, hatred of sin and a desire to pray and "feed" on the Bible as spiritual food. Most people who ask this question seriously have already answered it because apart from the work of the Holy Spirit they would not be concerned about such things.(Matt.5:6; Rom.8:5-8)

- c) The witness of the Holy Spirit. He is able to give us an inner conviction that we are children of God (Rom. 8:16)

The order is most important because our assurance must first be grounded on what God says rather than on anything in ourselves.

CHALLENGES from STUDY 23

 What, if any, are the hindrances you feel to your coming to faith in Jesus Christ?

 What, if any, are the hindrances to your being baptised as a believer in Jesus Christ?

 What are you going to do about these problems?

 What text has been especially meaningful to you during these sessions? Make a point of learning it thoroughly and taking it to heart as your own.

 What Now?

ACTION

 Go and speak to one of the leaders in the church you attend to whom you find it easiest to open your heart.

APPENDICES

1   Key to Bible book name abbreviations

2   Daily Bible reading schemes and notes

3   A list of basic Bible readings

KEY TO ABBREVIATIONS USED FOR BIBLE BOOKS

Old Testament

Gen.	Genesis
Exod.	Exodus
Lev.	Leviticus
Num.	Numbers
Deut.	Deuteronomy
Josh.	Joshua
Judg.	Judges
Ruth	Ruth
1 Sam.	1 Samuel
2 Sam.	2 Samuel
1 Kings	1 Kings
2 Kings	2 Kings
1 Chr.	1 Chronicles
2 Chr.	2 Chronicles
Ezra	Ezra
Neh.	Nehemiah
Esth.	Esther
Job	Job
Ps.	Psalms
Prov.	Proverbs
Eccles.	Ecclesiastes
S of S.	Song of Songs
Isa.	Isaiah
Jer.	Jeremiah
Lam.	Lamentations
Ezek.	Ezekiel
Dan.	Daniel
Hosea	Hosea
Joel	Joel
Amos	Amos
Obad.	Obadiah
Jonah	Jonah
Micah	Micah
Nahum	Nahum
Hab.	Habakkuk
Zeph.	Zephaniah
Hag.	Haggai
Zech.	Zechariah
Mal.	Malachi

New Testament

Matt.	Matthew
Mark	Mark
Luke	Luke
John	John
Acts	Acts
Rom.	Romans
1 Cor.	1 Corinthians
2 Cor.	2 Corinthians
Gal.	Galatians
Eph.	Ephesians
Phil.	Philippians
Col.	Colossians
1 Thess.	1 Thessalonians
2 Thess.	2 Thessalonians
1 Tim.	1 Timothy
2 Tim.	2 Timothy
Titus	Titus
Philem.	Philemon
Heb.	Hebrews
James	James
1 Peter	1 Peter
2 Peter	2 Peter
1 John	1 John
2 John	2 John
3 John	3 John
Jude	Jude
Rev.	Revelation

AV	*Authorised Version*
RAV	*Revised Authorised Version*
NKJV	*New King James Version*
NIV	*New International Version*

DAILY BIBLE READING SCHEMES AND NOTES
ARE AVAILABLE FROM:

Geneva Bible Notes: Notes for study and meditation

Grace Publications Trust
The Christian Bookshop
Sevenoaks Road
Pratts Bottom
Orpinton, Kent
BR6 7SQ
Tel: 01689 854117

Discover: Bible reading notes for young people

Discover Publications
Arisaig
Crowborough Hill
Crowborough
East Sussex
TN6 2EA

Scripture Union: Provide schemes for various ages and stages of
spiritual experience and requirements

Scripture Union
130 City Road
London
EC1V 2NJ

Every Day With Jesus: Daily Bible readings and notes

CWR Waverley
Abbey House
Waverley Lane
Farnham
Surrey
GU9 8EP

NOTE: The schemes vary in style and usefulness. If possible obtain samples and seek advice
before deciding which to use

LIST OF BASIC BIBLE READINGS

Genesis	Ch 1-2	Creation
"	Ch 3	Sin came into the world
"	Ch 4-11	Nations were founded
"	Ch 12-50	The Hebrew nation formed
Exodus	Ch 1-11	Slavery in Egypt
"	Ch 12-19	Release from slavery – the Passover
"	Ch 20	The ten commandments
Joshua	Ch 1-8	Entry into the promised land
1 Samuel	Ch 16:1-13	David made king
Isaiah	Ch 53	The death of Christ predicted
Matthew	Ch 1-28	The birth, life, death & resurrection of Jesus Christ
John	Ch 1-5	The Son of God
Acts	Ch 1-17	The Spirit and the church
Romans	Ch 1-3	The way of salvation
Ephesians	Ch 2:1-10	The making of a Christian
"	Ch 5-6	Christian Living
Hebrews	Ch 11	The life of faith
2 Peter	Ch 3	The end of the world
Psalms	1	Godly Living
"	23	Humble Trust
"	51	Repentance
"	84	Joy in the Lord
"	103	Thanksgiving

NOTE: Read these passages two or three times and then move to one of the Bible reading schemes